Everyday Violence against Black and Latinx LGBT Communities

Everyday Violence against Black and Latinx LGBT Communities

Siobhan Brooks

LEXINGTON BOOKS
Lanham • Boulder • New York • London

Published by Lexington Books
An imprint of The Rowman & Littlefield Publishing Group, Inc.
4501 Forbes Boulevard, Suite 200, Lanham, Maryland 20706
www.rowman.com

6 Tinworth Street, London SE11 5AL, United Kingdom

British Library Cataloguing in Publication Information Available

Library of Congress Control Number: 2020943838

ISBN 978-1-4985-7575-1 (cloth)
ISBN 978-1-4985-7577-5 (pbk)
ISBN 978-1-4985-7576-8 (electronic)

Contents

Acknowledgments

There are many people who made this book possible. First I would like to thank all of my interviewees who took time out of their busy schedules to speak with me. A special thank you to Bamby Salcedo and Charles B. Brack for sharing your work in the community with me and expanding our solutions of how to curb violence against LGBT Black and Latinx communities. I am grateful for the interview I was able to obtain with Pulse massacre survivor, Angel Torres, who took time to recount the frightening details of the shooting with me. He shared his firsthand experience of the courage of fellow survivors and the systemic failure of law enforcement.

I am equally thankful to have interviewed both Nikole Parker and Roxy Santiago of the onePULSE Foundation, and learn how they are helping transform their community in Orlando, Florida and by extension our nation. I am forever indebted to Sylvia Guerrero, whom I met in 2007 at a screening of the documentary, "Trained in the Ways of Men," at the Castro Theater in San Francisco. Over the years I have invited Sylvia to speak to college students about the murder trial of her daughter, Gwen Araujo, and she has done so graciously in the midst of pain and hardship. I can't thank her enough, and offer this book as a small gesture of gratitude. I have much respect for the political insight of Patrisse Cullors, co-founder of Black Lives Matter. I am thankful to her for sharing her political views and collation building techniques to work for social change across difference. Her insight was invaluable to this project. My friendships with Dr. Eddy Francisco Alvarez and Robert Quintana Hopkins sustained me during this project, and I am grateful for their love, support, and time.

This book benefited from the unconditional love of my spouse, Alejandra Luna. Their support and belief of my work continue to carry me when the road ahead is not clear. *Te amo mucho siempre.* Our furry kids, Bowie and Ziggy, left their mark on this book also.

I owe thanks to my acquisitions editor, Kasey Beduhn, at Rowman & Littlefield who reached out to me regarding the project. Thank you for your patience and belief in my ideas for this book. It really would not have been possible without your insight.

I dedicate this book to the memory of Dr. Lamar Jerome Smith (1985–2018) who unexpectedly passed away in 2018. Lamar was a magnificent soul. He was a psychologist and activist here in Orange County, California who spearheaded LGBT therapeutic services and other resources to an underserved population. I will always be grateful for his friendship, brilliance, and for taking time to speak in my Black LGBT class at Cal State Fullerton. You will always be remembered for your generosity.

Lastly, I acknowledge all the survivors of violence in its multiple forms and look forward to a day when this will no longer be the case.

Introduction

I began to think about hate crimes against LGBT Black and Latinx[1] people after the Pulse nightclub shooting in 2016 that killed fifty people in Orlando, Florida. Prior to the shooting, I felt that some progress was being made regarding LGBT issues: images of queer people of color were becoming accepted within mainstream media, gay marriage had passed within the United States, and many workplaces prior to the 2020 Supreme Court decision included nondiscrimination clauses against LGBT people, among other marginal statuses (i.e., race, disability, gender, and so on). I thought about my own life as a Black lesbian with my spouse, a gender-nonconforming Latinx identified person, as we reside in Orange County, California—a place known for its conservatism. In fact, a few months before the shooting, I was commenting to my spouse that for the most part we felt accepted by our neighbors, our jobs, and overall we felt safe holding hands in public.

Then Pulse happened, and I started rethinking what I had thought was true about my own life, and that of many Black and Latinx LGBT people, especially transgender women, who remained marginalized in spite of these civil rights gains. I also began to notice how the Pulse massacre was covered in the media and who was talking about it and who was not. Most mainstream gay and lesbian organizations in Orlando, and nationally, described it as a "gay" hate crime; some underscored the race of the shooter being of Middle Eastern descent, and having possible ties with ISIS—a viewpoint seen as advancing Islamophobia. In some publications, such as *The Advocate,* the race of the attacker was noted, while the fact that the victims were Latinx and Black was ignored. This erasure mirrors the marginalization of people of color within mainstream white gay and lesbian movements and also supports the stereotype that queer issues are not people of color issues. Similarly, some mainstream white gay and lesbian social media groups failed to mention the

1

shooting at all, instead focusing on the ISIS shooting in France that killed a police officer, which supports claims of Islamophobia in how the Pulse shooting was perceived.

The consequences of this media coverage were found on my Facebook page—which is filled with posts from progressive Black, white, and Latino/a activists and scholars. Most of the people who expressed outrage on my page were other queer people of color and some queer white people; hardly any of the straight identified people of color or white people had much to say about this mass shooting. Many queer people of color called out what appeared to be a "heterosexual silence" regarding the shooting of forty-nine mostly queer identified Black and Latinx people. The silence came from people who usually post about police shootings of Black and brown men by the police. When challenged on social media by queer Black and Latinx people regarding their silence, some replied that they just didn't know what to say. Some were reluctant to post for fear of being labeled as gay. Others had mixed emotions, including some queer identified Middle Eastern people, who felt the focus on the race of the shooter underscored racism against Islam. Further reports stated that Omar Mateen originally wanted to shoot Disney Springs (Forbes 2003) but there were too many police there (Cullen 2018).

There was also speculation that he was a closeted gay man, and had a Grindr account—we may never know the reasons Mateen committed this violent act, but we know that it is in a long line of history of violence against Black and Latinx communities and LGBT communities. Overall, many within the queer people of color social media community viewed these lack of responses as a cop out. The twenty-six people I interviewed for this book shared this fear and disappointment in what they perceived as a lack of urgency concerning the lives of LGBT Black and Latinx people.

I interviewed Dr. Eddy Francisco Alvarez Jr., a professor of Chicano/a Studies at Cal State Fullerton University, who shared the following after the Pulse nightclub shooting:

> Right after the shooting at Pulse my heart was broken knowing that this homophobic/transphobics act had taken place. I expected others on FB [Facebook]—queer and not—to be enraged and blowing up their FB post like they did when other shootings or tragedies happened. I was saddened, disappointed, and angry that people seemed to be indifferent. I noticed many of my heterosexual identified friends and family were not posting anything. I posted several things about how I felt and then some people commented on my post saying they that were in shock, or that silence didn't mean they weren't upset, but there wasn't the same type of outage. Sadly, it was many Latino/a and other folks of color who were silent. It felt like these queer lives didn't matter, and as an extension of them—like I didn't matter.

While my Facebook page may not be the most representative source to gauge support for LGBT Black and Latinx people, it is telling because Facebook is an outlet where current political issues and thoughts are circulated. I realized in these Facebook exchanges that queer issues were still not viewed as Black and Latino/a issues, largely because of how they are framed—as white. While people may not be verbally expressing anti-LGBT views, their silence about the violence that happens against us speaks volumes. In moments like this, I am reminded of the following words of Dr. Martin Luther King, "In the end, we will remember not the words of our enemies, but the silence of our friends" (King 1968). In other words, the silence functions as a form of symbolic violence, which reinforces the devaluing of LGBT Black and Latinx lives within social movements, regarding who gets to be mourned in times of everyday systemic death.

EVERYDAY FORMS OF VIOLENCE

On September 17, 2019, Ed Buck, a businessman and LGBT political activist, was arrested and charged for battery and maintaining a drug house. Since 2017 three Black men have died at his house as a result of being injected with methamphetamine (Branson-Potts 2019). The intersectional politics in this case underscores life on the fringes for many queer Black and Latinx people, and the overrepresentation of them in hate crime cases. Ed Buck is a white gay wealthy man and his victims were Black and poor, including the last man who escaped his home after being drugged. This man is now homeless. Many would not see this as an example of a hate crime because the victims and the perpetrator are gay—but the men were targeted also because of race.

According to Doug Meyer (2015) contrary to what's portrayed in the media, most LGBT hate crime victims are people of color. What has been understudied is the degree to which queer Black and Latinx people experience everyday forms of violence from institutions within and outside of their communities, based on sexual orientation and/or gender identity, and racial violence from within white LGBT communities. The murders of transgender women of color illustrate these intersecting forms of everyday hatred and violence. Hate is not always in the form of overt violence and slurs, but institutionalized within our social fabric as racism, sexism, heterosexism, and transphobia resulting in microaggressions (Nadal 2019), and discrimination leading to underemployment, religious persecution, educational marginalization, and lack of health care.

In *Everyday Violence against Black and Latinx LGBT Communities,* I explore everyday forms of institutional violence and how this can result in physical violence and social death using interviews and data analysis. For example, there is a lot of media images of stories of Black and Latinx trans women being murdered, without discussions of structural changes within health care, housing, and employment, which would help to eradicate the violence they face as a result of their marginalization.

I use the framework of everyday violence, which was first coined by Nancy Scheper-Hughes (1992), to highlight social indifference to suffering in analyzing violence in Brazil among mothers and children. I extend her analysis to explore the everyday ways LGBT Black and Latinx people experience social and institutional violence that lead up to physical assault. I argue that when we explore the ways LGBT Black and Latinx people are impacted by hate crimes, and overall institutional violence (religious, educational, and medical) and communities (family, friends, colleagues), we can find possible solutions to curbing violence against LGBT Black and Latinx people. I focus on Black and Latinx LGBT people because they have high numbers of hate crimes against them and experience similar forms of racial segregation. I also focus on the exclusion of LGBT Black and Latinx people within their racial group more than the larger white society because most Blacks and Latinx people live among their racial group, not among white people. Therefore, the actions of institutions within Black and Latinx communities have a direct impact on them along with the racism and hetero/cisgender[2] supremacy of the larger society.

I am also interested in the impact of physical violence in LGBT Black and Latinx communities who are often reported as experiencing higher hate crimes, but there are few scholarly studies exploring what multiple forms of violence do to a community, and what resiliency looks like.

According to FBI statistics, hate crimes have increased by 4.6 percent since Trump was sworn into office in 2016. Stephen Rushin and Edwards Griffin argue that hate crimes rose with the election of Donald Trump who spoke ill of immigrants, referred to Mexican men as rapists, and created a political and social climate for people of color, and LGBT people of various races, to be attacked (Rushin and Griffin 2018).

In addition to violence hate is institutionalized against LGBT Black and Latinx people via laws and policies. Recently, the Supreme Court decided that Title VII does apply to LGBT people in the workplace, which is a huge step toward curbing institutional marginalization. Yet, the Supreme Court also decided that they would not revisit the Qualified Immunity doctrine regarding police officers, thus allowing them to exercise abusive violence against marginalized communities. The U.S. Department of Health and Human Service's policy has restricted health care for transgender people, which hopefully the Supreme Court decision can reverse.

These types of decisions result in LGBT Black and Latinx people being vulnerable to violence because of economic marginality, leading to them being housing insecure, and in the criminal justice system. These laws are examples of everyday violence. How do queer Black and Latinx people take care of themselves and their communities after hearing about or experiencing physical violence given the limited resources they are working with? How are institutions that serve Black and Latinx communities implicated in violence?

In *Everyday Violence against Black and Latinx LGBT Communities*, I aim to answer these questions by examining everyday violence and community response, in the following settings: family, workplace, and institutions (i.e., health care, religious, and educational spaces). I also explore the impact of violence on mental health, activism, and restorative justice practices of Black and Latinx LGBT community members. I conclude by arguing that by examining everyday violence, how it disrupts communities, and the challenges experienced by people and their loved ones who survived violence, we can develop strategies to help eradicate hate crimes and overall structural violence. We can provide queer Black and Latinx people resources to survive, and live without the fear of violence that is not rooted in more hate crime laws, but institutional and cultural change.

METHODS AND OUTLINE OF THE BOOK

It's not easy to talk about hate crimes and violence, especially in cases of murder. Hence, because of the sensitive nature of the topic, I did most of my interviewees for the book via the snowball method, by asking people within my network, and then being connected to other interested people. I gained IRB approval from my university and offered gift cards to my interviewees. I had to be careful how I approached people; for example, some members of trans women of color organizations felt that to interview trans women about their experiences of violence with only a gift card as compensation was exploitative. I understood this viewpoint, even though this is a standard practice within social science research regarding payments for interviews, and I am grateful for the interviews I was able to get. I interviewed a total of twenty-six people for the project: Thirteen Black identified people (one Black Latinx individual), and twelve Latinx identified people; two gender-queer identified people. Twenty-two non-trans identified individuals, one gender-nonconforming, and three trans women.

I used pseudonyms for my interviewees except for the following individuals: Dr. Eddy Francisco Alvarez, Angel Torres, Bamby Salcedo, J. P. Howard, Charles B. Brack, Patrisse Cullors, Marta Cunningham, and Sylvia Guerrero. All eight participants wanted to use their real names so I code their responses under their real name. Sylvia Guerrero is a personal friend of mine and has been very open about the murder trial of her trans daughter, Gwen

Araujo. The interview material with Sylvia is based on a conservation I had with her on the phone as I did most of my interviews via phone, except for Bamby, whom I interviewed at her Los Angeles office.

Some of the questions I asked my interviewees were: Have you experienced a hate crime? If so, what was the response from law enforcement? Family? Friends? Did you receive the support you needed? If you were not a survivor of an attack, how did you feel hearing about violence happening in the community? How have you experienced discrimination in education, job, health care, and/or religious communities? What do you think should be done legally and socially to end hate crimes and structural marginalization?

Chapter 1 explores the legal framework and limitations of what constitutes a hate crime. LGBT Black and Latinx people experience high rates of hate crimes, but the criminal justice system has not always been a source of justice for them. Hate crime laws often target people of color more than whites, and don't focus on the structural problems, which results in hate crimes, but instead individual acts of violence. Chapter 2 investigates the intersections of identities of race, class, and gender identity when exploring hate crimes and everyday violence against LGBT Black and Latinx people with a focus on the cases of CeCe McDonald, Sakia Gunn, and Zoraida Reyes, and Latisha King.[3] Chapter 3 moves the conversation from hate crimes being done by strangers upon LGBT Black and Latinx people, to everyday violence within the family and larger communities. This chapter provides analysis of marginalization of LGBT Black and Latinx people within families; race-based social movements, educational, religious, and employment sectors. I argue that an increase in hate crime laws will not end the violence against LGBT Black and Latinx people until there is structural institutional change.

Chapter 4 examines the community and family impact of hate crimes against LGBT Black and Latinx people. Families and survivors of anti-LGBT-related hate crimes experience family isolation, financial hardship, and community stigma because of homo/transphobia. This stigma is evident in families having difficulties finding a church service for their murdered loved one, along with lack of legal intervention against preventing violence, and victim blaming of those who survived hate crimes, especially transgender people of color. Chapter 5 considers the impact of hate crimes on the mental health of queer Black and Latinx people, and how this affects their activism. I investigate issues of PTSD, forgiveness, dissociation, self-care, and activism. Some people were traumatized by hate crimes and could no longer work, suffering economic instability as a result. Parents such as Sylvia Guerrero found a way to forgive individuals for the murder of their child if they have shown remorse. Some community members completely dissociate themselves from a hate crime incident especially if it happened to someone else, sometimes to the point of blaming the victim for what has happened to them. This is the case when trans women are murdered while engaging in sex work.

However, hate crimes can mobilize people into action and create community, which was seen in the aftermath of the Pulse shooting. Some activists fight to be more out as Black and Latinx LGBT people in their workplaces, health care facilities, schools, and religious institutions.

Chapter 6 explores the meaning of justice for survivors of hate crimes, and community members who lost loved ones to hate crimes. I focus on restorative justice models as a method that LGBT Black and Latinx community members preferred to the prison system. Many Black and Latinx communities do not have positive relationships with law enforcement, and for LGBT Black and Latinx people that distrust is underscored by the transphobia, racism, and homophobia within the criminal justice system. Similar to survivors of domestic violence, survivors of LGBT-related hate crimes that used the criminal justice system to report a hate crime, are not convinced that the system will keep them safe from the perpetrator(s).

Some participants believed that in certain cases people who commit hate crimes should be separated from society, but that most perpetrators needed education and rehabilitation, so that they could understand the harm they caused LGBT Black and Latinx communities. In this chapter, I also critique the tacit of shaming as a form of punishment because often LGBT people are murdered out of shame (i.e., cisgender men who are shamed for dating trans women). Instead, I focus on types of community justice that are less about crime and punishment, and more about increasing institutional support and resources for Black and Latinx communities. Examples of this type of support would be in areas of housing, employment, education, religion, and health care. In educational settings, Black and Latinx students do not feel safe in the classroom or on school grounds, as a result of bullying and absence of their identity in the curriculum. Many Black and Latinx youth, especially trans youth, are homeless resulting from discrimination within families. Black and Latinx LGBT adults can experience housing insecurity because of racism, homophobia, and/or transphobia within employment, thus limiting their ability to economically provide for themselves, and discrimination in housing markets.

In the field of health care, many LGBT Black and Latinx people face challenges to accessing health care, from lack of health insurance, racism of medical professionals, dearth of training serving Black /Latinx LGBT communities, and institutionalized homo/transphobia during patient intakes. Black and Latinx trans people are often refused hormones, the language in doctor's offices is outdated and heteronormative, and therapist need to be trained on the mental health needs of Black and Latinx people.

Lastly, religious reform is needed to eradicate hate crimes against Black and Latinx LGBT people, especially since churches play a major role in community organizing and the sharing of resources. Churches and religious leaders hold power and influence in these communities concerning what type of people are valued in Black and Latinx communities. Some churches have become more LGBT friendly, but many churches are still traditionally Christian and/or Catholic with pastors and/or priests teaching negative messages about LGBT people. These negative teachings in churches are one of the main justifications for hate crimes within Black and Latinx LGBT communities. Similar to educational spaces and health care industries, churches must become places of love and support for LGBT people—not a place that encourages hate crimes to occur against this group. While it has always been true that queer Black and Latinx people have existed within religious institutions under a "don't ask, don't tell" policy, in order to eradicate hate crimes, LGBT people must not only be tolerated, but accepted as part of the larger community of Black and Latinx civic society.

In sum, unless our society deals with the institutional aspects of hate crimes against LGBT Black and Latinx people, not only as individual acts of hate, we will not move forward. This book is timely especially during the presidency of Donald Trump, which has fostered a climate of hate against various groups of people (immigrants, LGBT groups, women, Black people). In this political atmosphere it is LGBT Black and Latinx people that exist at the intersections of these hateful acts, and hold the greatest hope for structural change.

NOTES

1. I use the term Latinx to distinguish between Latino/a to imply the gender-neutral term.

2. The term cisgender is used to describe people who identify with their assigned sex. I find this term to also be problematic when applying it to people who have been marginalized with gender because of race (i.e., Black people; Black women not being treated like the normative category of woman). In spite of these criticisms, I use the term throughout the book when discussing trans people and non-trans people.

3. I use the name King went by at the time of death to honor their identity.

Chapter 1

Legal Framework of Hate Crimes

The term "hate crime" originated in the 1980s, describing violence against LGBT and people of color (Ramirez et al. 2017). Hate crimes against LGBT individuals came into national discourse via the murder of Matthew Shepard in 1998.[1] Since the murder of Shepard, LGBT activists have organized to strengthen hate crime laws concerning violence against LGBT people. According to the National Gay and Lesbian Task Force, states with hate crime laws including sexual orientation and/or gender identity are Arizona, California, Colorado, Connecticut, Delaware, District of Columbia, Florida, Hawaii, Illinois, Iowa, Kansas, Kentucky, Louisiana, Maine, Massachusetts, Maryland, Minnesota, Missouri, Nebraska Nevada, New Jersey, New Mexico, New Hampshire, New York, Oregon, Rhode Island, Tennessee, Texas, Vermont, Washington, and Wisconsin (National Gay and Lesbian Task Force 2013). Yet, twenty states do not enhance penalties for crimes regarding sexual orientation, and thirty-four states don't have increased penalties for crimes involving transgender people. This is after the 2015 historic Supreme Court decision legalizing gay marriage in all states. While the United States has made gains in LGBT equality, discrimination and violence against LGBT populations, especially LGBT people of color, remain. The violence that LGBT Black and Latinx people, especially youth, face is not only by strangers, but by family members as well.

For example, in 1999 Steen Fenrich, a nineteen-year-old-gay Black man from Queens, New York, was murdered and dismembered by his white stepfather who carved the words, "Gay Nigger Number One," and his social security number into his skull (Herszenhorn 2000).

On May 13, 2013, an eight-year-old Gabriel Fernandez was murdered by his mother and her boyfriend in Palmdale, California, because they thought he was gay (Dillon 2018). They tortured him, fracturing his skull, broke his ribs, burned his skin, knocked his teeth out, and shot BB pellets into his groin. Gabriel's mother's boyfriend, Isauro Aguirre is believed to have tortured Gabriel because he suspected he was gay (ibid.). At the trial for Gabriel's murder, his mother Pearl Sinthia Fernandez received life in prison, while her boyfriend was sentenced to death.[2]

Also, in California a ten-year-old Anthony Avalos was murdered by his caregivers for being gay. Avalos died from head injuries and had cigarette burns over his body. According to the *Los Angeles Times*, Avalos had recently stated that he liked boys, and an investigation is underway to determine if homophobia played a role in his death. His mother, Heather Barron, and her boyfriend, Kareem Leiva, have not been charged with his death—in spite of numerous calls to DCFS from teachers concerning child abuse against Anthony and his six siblings (Therolf 2018).

In Atlanta, Georgia, on March 20, 2016, Martin Blackwell poured boiling hot water onto the bodies of Marquez Tolbert, 21, and his boyfriend Anthony Gooden, twenty-four. The couple was sleeping at Anthony's mother's house, and Blackwell was her boyfriend (Hauser 2016). Mr. Tolbert spent ten days in the hospital suffering severe burns requiring skin grafting, and being placed in a medically induced coma. Blackwell was sentenced to forty years in prison for assault and battery, but not a hate crime because Georgia does not have hate crime laws (Levy and Levy 2017).

The above cases involving family members are important in underscoring that anti-LGBT violence does not occur only among strangers, but within families. When anti-LGBT violence is committed within families, it doesn't always legally qualify as a hate crime, albeit the violence and targeting of individuals because they are queer is in alignment with the definition of hate crimes. They have more in common with honor killings (Asquith and Fox 2015).

STATISTICS ON HATE CRIMES

According to the 2016 Hate Crime Report of Los Angeles County Commission on Human Relations, 94 percent of crimes motivated by gender identity were against transgender women—69 percent were Latina and 14 percent were Black compared with 17 percent being white. In cases where suspects were identified, 51 percent were Black men and 43 percent were Latino. Nationally, in 2017 twenty-five transgender people were murdered, 84 percent were people of color, and 80 percent were women mostly under thirty-five years of age, and over half of the victims lived in the South with the fewest legal protections for LGBT people.[3] Many of the murders were not classified as hate crimes, and often the victims were misgendered. As a result of this violence, gay rights activists fought to have hate crime laws introduced in various states to provide protection and legal accountability to LGBT people. The institutionalization of hate crime laws and enhanced penalties, such as the death penalty, has divided LGBT communities; while some people feel that there should be stricter crime control laws regarding anti-LGBT violence, many feel that the death penalty is not the answer (Kohn 2002). This is one of many critiques of current hate crime legislation regarding LGBT populations.

Hate crime activists have been successful at legally naming violence against marginalized groups and attempting to provide legal protection to targeted groups (Spade and Willse 2000). An example of this is the murder trial of Gwen Araujo, a Latinx transgender teen killed by four men in Northern California after they discovered she was transgender. Two of the defendants were convicted of second-degree murder, but not hate crime charges, the other two pleaded to voluntary manslaughter, with the trans panic defense used in one of the trails. Activism against this ruling resulted in the Gwen Araujo Justice for Victims Act,[4] signed by former California governor Arnold Schwarzenegger, which prohibits juries from using gay/trans panic defenses.[5] While this law does not pertain to hate crimes per se, it does decrease the chances of LGBT murder defendants receiving lesser sentencing based on gay/trans defenses. The Araujo case also educated many media sources on how to properly address transgender people regarding pronouns, since many transgender people are misgendered in media sources.

However, many scholars of queer and critical race theory question the effectiveness of hate crime laws, and argue that the benefits of such laws remain to be seen (Meyers 2014; Spade 2013).

CRITIQUE OF LGBT-RELATED HATE CRIME LAWS

If someone experiences a hate crime, they may not report it to the police because they could be blamed; they could be undocumented and scared of deportation.

Bamby Salcedo, President and CEO of the Trans Latina Coalition

In spite of the beliefs that hate crime laws reduce violence toward LGBT people, this is not always the case. According to Doug Meyer (2014), the institutionalization of hate crime laws unfairly penalizes people of color and working class people being that Blacks and Latinos are often treated unfairly by the criminal justice system—hate crime laws expand the criminal justice system targeting against people of color. Additionally, Blacks and Latinx individuals are disproportionately affected by anti-LGBT hate crimes, and would be less likely to be protected by hate crime laws since they are not protected by law enforcement and often abused by the criminal justice system.

Another critique of hate crime laws is that they don't address cultural and structural marginalization of LGBT people and people of color, instead focusing on individual acts of violence directed toward these groups (Spade and Willse 2000). For example, police violence, unemployment, homelessness, lack of health care, and educational erasure are not viewed as hate crimes; it is only when an act of violence is committed that the act is classified as a hate crime (ibid.). In other words, the marginalization of people of color and queer people is normal, and legally it is not a crime to hate someone. According to the FBI website section "Defining Hate Crime":

> A hate crime is a traditional offense like murder, arson, or vandalism with an added element of bias. For the purposes of collecting statistics, the FBI has defined a hate crime as a "criminal offense against a person or property motivated in whole or in part by an offender's bias against a race, religion, disability, sexual orientation, ethnicity, gender, or gender identity." Hate itself is not a crime—and the FBI is mindful of protecting freedom of speech and other civil liberties. (FBI 2019)

Hence, it is not a crime for the state to foster a climate where groups of people are marginalized and hated in the form of the criminal justice system, which discriminates in arrest of people of color versus whites—but this same system is utilized to try and protect those marginalized groups from violence. Advocating for hate crime laws also ignores the activism of early queer movements, such as the 1969 Stonewall riots, which was a direct action against police harassment of queer people in clubs.

This contradiction between state violence and state protection is what makes hate crime laws ineffective in protecting LGBT people, especially people of color, from violence. Another problem with hate crime laws is the focus on a single identity responsible for why the person was targeted for violence—in the case of LGBT hate crimes it is sexual orientation/gender identity. For queer people of color other intersecting identities, such as race and class, play a role in why they are attacked (Meyer 2015). This single-issue focus on sexual orientation was seen in the Orlando Massacre of 2016 when media coverage only reported it as a "gay shooting" ignoring other marginal status markers of the victims and survivors of the Pulse shooting. Some white gay activists called for stricter hate crime and gun control laws, but not access to health care, housing, or employment—issues that affected the population at the Pulse nightclub (Ramirez 2017).

Another critique of hate crime laws is the notion of a perfect victim—white, cisgender, middle-class, able-bodied. Matthew Shepard emerged as the perfect hate crime victim,[6] and was able to have media coverage and activism around his death, while earlier a Black transgender woman was murdered and received very little media recognition (Loffreda 2000). This logic corresponds to ideas about a perfect rape victim that constructed white women as rape victims, and prevented Black women from being seen as worthy of protection from sexual violence from white men during the turn of the century, and resulted in Black men being viewed as rapist of white women (Davis 1982).

In addition to queer respectability politics, regarding who is worthy of being a victim, is the ranking of which lives matter, that is embedded in hate crime laws (Kohn 2002). According to Sally Kohn, "hate crime legislation actually runs counter to the interests of the GLBT movement. American criminal jurisprudence is based on categorization of people into two classes: those deemed worthy of the criminal law's protection and those deemed underserving . . ." (Kohn 2002: 1). Hence, the institutionalization of hate crime laws can create resentment within the larger society toward the very groups the law claims to protect. This is very evident when race is factored into how hate crime laws operate.

RACE-BASED HATE CRIME LAWS

On February 26, 2012, a seventeen-year-old Black male, Trayvon Martin, was walking home from a store when a twenty-eight-year-old neighborhood watch coordinator George Zimmerman, a mixed-race Latino, shot Martin, claiming self-defense, and viewing him as a suspicious person. In the aftermath of the shooting he was not arrested, and only after pressure from Martin's family and the community was an arrest made. In April of 2012, Zimmerman was charged with second-degree murder, and a trial began on June 10, 2013, concluding with a not guilty verdict on July 13, 2013. The U.S. Department of Justice stated that there was not enough evidence for Zimmerman to be charged with a hate crime prosecution (Berman and Horwitz 2015). The case sparked the Black Lives Matter movement bringing national and international attention on racial profiling and police brutality of Blacks by law enforcement. Yet, in spite of the media coverage of police violence against people of color, very few police officers were charged with murder, and none a hate crime. In fact, it has only been in 2017 that a police officer, Michael Slager, who shot and killed Walter Scott during a traffic stop, received a twenty-year prison sentence. But Slager was not convicted of a hate crime, since police violence doesn't constitute a hate crime, but rather officers doing their job.

For Black people legal measures to support their civil rights have their origins in the Reconstruction era, especially within the Thirteenth and

Fourteenth Amendments, and the Civil Rights Act of 1866, which provided criminal penalties against government officials restricting civil rights to newly freed slaves (Levin 2002). However, shortly after the Civil Rights Act, the Supreme Court challenged laws protecting Black citizenship by throwing out convictions. One of such cases emerging out of the Reconstruction Era, and interpreting the Civil Rights Act, was Blyew v. United States (Levin 2002).

In the case two white men in Kentucky, Blyew and Kennard, murdered a Black family (the Foster family) in response to the passage of the Fourteenth Amendment, two Black girls escaped as witnesses to the crime. Kentucky law did not allow testimony from Blacks against white people, and the case was moved to federal court with hopes of provoking the Civil Rights Act, which stated that, "Affecting persons who are denied, or cannot enforce in the courts or judicial tribunals of the State, or locality, where they may be, any of the rights secured to them by the first section of the act" (Civil Rights Act 1866). In other words, the case could be moved to federal courts to ensure protection of people's (in this case former slaves) civil rights.

However, the government moved it back to the courts of Kentucky arguing that the federal government did not have jurisdiction. Thus, the Supreme Court ruled that Blacks were prohibited to testify against whites, and that witnesses were not affected persons by the crime, since they did not directly experience it (Browne-Marshall 2013). In today's society, we understand what happened to the Foster family to be a hate crime, since the murder was race based, but in 1866 the Supreme Court did not view it this way.

Since the Foster case there has been an increase in advocating for hate crime laws, with hate crime activists arguing that they decrease violence and discrimination against LGBT people and people of color (Lawrence 1999). The most famous race-based case prompting hate crime legislation was the Texas murder of James Byrd Jr. in 1998.[7] In 2009, former President Obama signed the Matthew Shepard and James Byrd Jr. Hate Crime Prevention Act into law. Yet, in spite of Obama signing this act into law, hate crimes against people of color, and LGBT people, have not decreased. According to the FBI Hate Crime Statistics in 2009, there were 6,598 single-bias reported hate crime incidents, with 48.5 percent racially motivated, and 18.5 percent motivated by sexual orientation[8]; in 2010, there were 6,624 single-bias reported incidents, 47.3 racially motivated, and 19.3 by sexual orientation; in 2011, there were 6,216 single-bias reported incidents with 46.9 percent racially motivated, and 20.8 percent by sexual orientation.

In 2015 the year gay marriage was legalized, there were 5,818 single-bias incidents with 59.2 percent racially motivated, and 17.7 percent motivated by sexual orientation. In the last years of Obama presidency, there were 6,063 single-bias incidents, of which 57.5 percent were racially motivated, and 17.7 percent were motivated by sexual orientation (FBI Hate Crime Statistics).

These statistics illustrate that contrary to the intent of hate crime laws creating more tolerance in society for marginalized people, they in fact do the opposite, which is to create resentment toward marginalized groups by the larger society (Franklin 2002). The other issues these statistics highlight are that more media representation of marginalized groups does not decrease violence toward them (Fitzgerald 2017). For example, hate crimes against gay and lesbian people only slightly decreased from 2011 to 2015 when gay marriage was legalized, and the murders of transgender women of color have continued, even with Black transgender women, such as Laverne Cox and Janct Mock being visible in the media.

Similarly, during President Obama's term there was an increase in police murders of Black people, in spite of the nation having a Black president (Fakunle, Smiley, and Gomez 2017). The violence against Black people and LGBT people is continuous even in the age of new technology documenting forms of hatred—in fact technology has not curbed violence, but instead spreads it across the Internet, into newsfeeds, and Facebook posts.

DOCUMENTING HATE

On March 3, 1991, the nation viewed the beating of Rodney King, a Black man in Los Angeles who was pulled over by police for speeding. Initially, King refused to pull over, which led to a high-speed chase by six police officers: Tim and Melanie Singer, Stacey Koon, Lawrence Powell, Timothy Wind, Theodore Briseno, and Rolando Solano. When officers caught up King they beat him with batons and tasered him. George Holliday from his apartment captured the beatings on videotape.[9] Many Black people in the Los Angeles area, and the nation, have witnessed police brutality—but this was the first time someone videotaped what most Black people in urban areas have always experienced. Four officers were charged of assault, and a year later were acquitted of using excessive force; this led to riots in Los Angeles that lasted from April 29 to May 4, 1992 (Rabinowitz 2015). Many people felt that surely with video proof of police brutality, officers would be convicted of assault and excessive force. This has not been the case. Since the King riots, there has been an influx of Internet footage and cell phone videos in the era of the Black Lives Matter movement of police violence against people of color, especially Black men. The deaths of Eric Garner,[10] Philando Castile,[11] and George Floyd[12] were captured on cell phone; in spite of this evidence, officers were not convicted in the deaths of these men.

The history of documenting hatred of Black people for the purposes of social change has its roots in the most famous image of racial hatred, which was the 1955 lynching of Emmett Till in Mississippi. Till who was fourteen years old was from Chicago visiting relatives and killed by two white men after reportedly flirting with a white woman in a grocery store. His body was found in the Tallahatchie River, disfigured, and his eyes gouged out. His mother, Mamie Till, held an open casket funeral for her son to show the world the injustices Black people in the United States faced. The photo was epitomized as a symbol for the Civil Rights Movement; yet, the two murders accused of murdering Till were acquitted.

Similarly, the documentation of anti-LGBT hate crimes is going viral. On April 18, 2011, a white transgender woman, Chrissy Lee Polis was beaten by a group of Black teenage girls at a McDonald's in Rosedale, Maryland. A McDonald's employee videotaped the beating while other employees to intervene; some employees were heard laughing in the background. The video resulted in highlighting violence against transgender women and the girls were charged with assault and one pleaded guilty of a hate crime. This case reinforced some of the problems cited earlier with hate crime laws because the attackers were Black and the victim was white. Hence, this case supports the critique of involving more people of color in the criminal justice system, while ignoring the violence Black transgender women experience.[13]

Another example of the failure of proving an act of violence as a hate crime, even when filmed on video, is the murder of Anya Knee Parker. In October 2, 2014, Anya Knee Parker, a forty-seven-year-old Black transgender woman was shot and killed in Los Angeles in the early morning. She was walking down the street when three Latino men confronted her, tried to take her purse, and shot her in the head as she ran away; the murder was caught on surveillance video. The police described the shooting as a botched robbery and not a hate crime, though transgender community rights activists highlight the fact that transgender people are at increased risk for violence (Cruz 2014). Internationally, there was the February 15, 2017, murder of Dandara dos Santos, a forty-two-year-old transgender woman in Brazil, who was beaten, shot, and bashed with a stone by a group of men. The attack was caught on a cellphone and helped police identify some of the suspects, and bring awareness to violence against trans people in Brazil (Phillips 2017). But none was charged with a hate crime.

The use of technology in documenting state violence has helped bring visibility to the murders of Black women and Black LGBT people at the hands of the police. In spite of Black Lives Matter being founded by three Black women, two being queer, these are the very identities erased from discussions of police violence in Black communities. The campaign #SayHerName was coined from the African American Policy Forum in the wake of Sandra Bland's death in 2015. Since the creation of the #SayHerName movement the names of Black women and girls, such as seven-year-old Aiyana Stanley-Jones, who was killed by Detroit police, while sleeping on the couch; Natasha

McKenna who was tasered to death in a Virginia jail; and Rekia Boyd who was shot by police in Chicago, have circulated the Internet. Breonna Taylor was shot and killed during a no-knock search warrant in Louisville, Kentucky. Yet, the use of technology documenting these murders does not stop them.

Similarly, hate crimes and bullying against LGBT Black and brown people are also being documented via social media. Blake Brockington was an eighteen-year-old Black trans man who committed suicide in North Carolina. He was politically active, becoming the first transgender homecoming king in North Carolina. After dealing with depression and family rejection, he committed suicide by stepping out into traffic on a highway. Carl Joseph Walker-Hoover was an eleven-year-old Black boy who committed suicide via hanging in Springfield, Massachusetts after being bullied for being perceived as gay. Walker's suicide resulted in media coverage and school activism on behalf of his mother. However, the increase of technology in documenting bullying, and hate crimes, against LGBT people has not decreased them, in fact some perpetrators of these crimes post videos of the violence they are committing—this was the case with the murder of Dandara dos Santos.

The filming of violence against Black and queer bodies for commodification has its origins in lynchings and the burning of gay people during the colonial era. In the colonial United States, the first documented 1,646 cases of state murder against Black gay men was the case of Jan Creoli and Manuel Congo. Manuel Congo was a ten-year-old reported sodomized by Creoli, who was executed via being burned to death (Moguel, Ritchie, and Whitlock 2011).

In the late nineteenth century, more than 3,000 Black men, women, and children were lynched during the years 1880–1930 (Young 2005). In the article "The Black Body as Souvenir," Harvey Young argues that the practice of collecting the body parts of Black people is a key part of the act of lynching, as in the case of George Ward:

> It stages the transformation of the living body into a set of lifeless parts to be collected; the spectacle becomes materiality. In the case of George Ward, his lynching enacts his disappearance. The person and, indeed, the body (as a whole) recognized as Ward vanishes in the moments surrounding his death . . . his death creates souvenirs of his life. (Young 2005: 655)

Many scholars and activists criticized the racial terror reflective of Michael Brown's body being left on the ground with a sheet over it for hours where all the neighbors could see. Community residents felt his body was left there as an example by law enforcement of what can happen to all of them. In the article "Mike Brown's Shooting and Jim Crow Lynchings Have Too Much in Common," Isabel Wilkerson (2014) argues that the spectacle of his body lying in the street is reminiscent of Black bodies on display after a lynching. The images of dead Black bodies, while important for social activism, can also be commodified (Anderson 2015). In spite of the increase of video recordings of police violence against Black people, many online comments reveal that these men deserve to the shot, that they were criminals, and that police were just doing their job.

The hatred against Black victims of police violence is why respectability politics of whom is deemed an appropriate victim is upheld as a strategy to create sympathy, while excluding those groups deemed problematic (i.e., people with criminal convictions, people without college degrees, queer people of color). In spite of video footage of Black people sometimes being shot in the back by police, many still view them as criminal or doing something to bring on the violence (Obasogie and Newman 2016). In other words, with this strategy of respectability, the lives of Black people deemed upwardly mobile ranks higher than those viewed as underclass and deviant.

Similarly, in documenting anti-LGBT crimes, respectability politics is used to gather sympathy toward the victim, which reproduces notions of "good" queers versus "bad" queers. Unlike police violence against Black people, anti-LGBT violence is not captured on video, but more written about in the media.[14] The exceptions are murders of transgender women of color, such as Dandara dos Santos, or Anya Knee Parker, which were caught on video.

In other words, the video capturing of anti-LGBT and racial violence, while useful in bringing awareness, is not enough to ensure justice without a structural shift in the institutions that create violence against these groups. Similar with hate crime laws, the legal system alone cannot foster justice, and safety to marginal groups without root causes for violence being addressed.

CYBER-BULLYING, FREE SPEECH, AND HATE SPEECH

Another challenge to the success of hate crime laws is the issue of whether hate speech is freedom of speech. Similar to the fact that new technology has not decreased hate crimes, laws on hate speech fail to lessen harm against marginalized individuals. Advocates of hate crime laws view hate speech as something to be criminalized, because it often leads to actual violence against people of color and/or LGBT groups. This view is prevalent within school and universities where anti-LGBT hate speech has led to suicide, such as the case of Tyler Clementi (Waldman 2012). However, if the root of bullying in schools isn't addressed, the behavior will continue. According to C. J. Pascoe in her book *Dude, You're a Fag*, which focused on antigay bullying in high school, she accounted for numerous examples of antigay discourse, or what she termed "fag discourse," a process of how boys punished failed performances of masculinity, and the lack of response from faculty and administrators (Pascoe 2007). Since the publication of the book, she argues in the preface to the updated book that the fag discourse has moved into the Internet (Pascoe 2012).

The move of anti-LGBT hate speech onto the Internet has produced new legal challenges concerning hate crime laws. These challenges are noted in Ari Erza Waldman's article "Tormented: Antigay Bullying in Schools," where states such as Massachusetts have recently passed anti-bullying laws to include criminalization such as jail time.[15] In other states, legal actions have included state tort laws, Title VII, and Manslaughter charges for bullying resulting in death (Waldman 2012). However, the problem with these laws is that it is hard to prove who is guilty of manslaughter when cyber-bullying is involved—it could be a number of people. It's also hard to prove that bullying causes suicide (ibid.).

Advocates of hate speech as free speech argue that restrictions on any kind of speech are violations of the First Amendment; this was the court's decision in *R.A.V. v. St. Paul*, where a Black family in St. Paul Minnesota was terror-ized by a white skinhead placing a burning cross outside their home (Cowan et al. 2002). The city's ordinance ruled it to be a bias motivated act based on race, while the Supreme Court ruled the ordinance unconstitutional. This decision deterred punishment for hate crimes in the city (Thompson 1994). However, some scholars argue that infringements of First Amendment rights, including hate speech, contribute disproportionately to inner city students being punished, and expelled from school (Ross 2016: 719). Under these circumstances students refusing to pledge allegiance to the flag (Dane 1943), wear T-Shirts promoting or discouraging LGBT rights, protesting, and using offensive rap lyrics can be suspended and part of the school-to-prison pipe-line (Ross 2016: 728). Hence, similar to hate crime laws in general, criminal-ization does not address the root of hate speech, and contributes to the prison industrial complex.

CONCLUSION

The fight for tougher hate crime laws, including on hate speech, while suc-cessful in bringing awareness to the issue, won't stop it. This is true when analyzing the impact of hate crime laws on LGBT people of color. Albeit LGBT people of color comprise the highest numbers of hate crime cases, most are not advocating for harsher hate crime laws, but instead access to issues, such as health care, employment, police violence, homelessness, immigration, educational resources, and reforming of religious institu-tions. Most hate crime laws unfairly target the people most affected by hate

crimes—LGBT communities of color. The criminal justice system disproportionately punishes people of color, especially Blacks, for crimes assumed to
be against white victims (i.e., gay bashing). This framework imagines Black
and Latinos only as heterosexual and gay victims of hate crimes as middle
class and white.

Similarly, technology, such as cell phones and body cameras, has not produced a decrease in hate crimes and police violence against LGBT communities of color. In some cases technology (i.e., Internet, Webcams, Facebook)
has been used to bully and harass queer people, especially high school
students, with some of these cases being protected by the First Amendment
as freedom of speech. The criminalization of hate speech, like hate crimes,
affects inner city students more, creating a "school-to-prison" pipeline.

Instead, a more useful approach to ending violence against Black and
Latinx LGBT communities is investing in social systems, such as health
care, employment, and housing to provide them with the resources to be self-
actualizing and integrating into society. Educational systems can incorporate
LGBT and Ethnic Studies into K-12 curriculum. While media representation
is important in creating acceptance for marginalized communities, it cannot
occur without a change in the social systems that marginalize these groups
to begin with.

NOTES

1. Matthew Shepard was a white gay twenty-one-year-old male who was murdered in Laramie after meeting two men, Aaron McKinney and Russell Henderson at
a lounge. They offered Shepard a ride home and to beat and pistol-whip him, tying
him to a fence where he eventually died after being taken to the hospital and placed
on life support. The men who murdered him were convicted of murder. His death
sparked LGBT activism regarding hate crime legislation in the United States.

2. The Netflix documentary, "The Trials of Gabriel Fernandez" explores this
case more.

3. A Time to Act, Human Rights Campaign Report and Trans People of Color
Coalition. 2016.

4. "Gwen Araujo Justice for Victims Act." *California Legislative Information*,
September 28, 2006.

5. The gay panic defense was also used in the murder of Lawrence King by
stating that King, who was a transgender youth, was bullying Brandon McInterney,
and prompted him to shoot King twice in the head during a computer class. *Time
Magazine*, 2008.

6. Matthew Shepard was HIV positive but this fact was downplayed in the media.

7. James Byrd Jr. was a forty-nine-year-old Black man in Jasper, Texas who was
dragged from behind a pick-up truck by three men: Shawn Berry, Lawrence Russell
Brewer, and John King. Byrd accepted a ride from them where he has beaten and

dragged 1.5 miles. He died when his right arm and head were severed when his body hit a curb. The men were convicted of murder, with Brewer and King receiving the death penalty and Berry life in prison.

8. I focused on hate crimes motivated by race and sexual orientation bias because they constituted the largest categories of hate crimes.

9. Report of the Independent Commission on the Los Angeles Police Department: p. 6. 1991.

10. Eric Garner was a forty-three-year-old Black man in New York City who was approached by police on suspicion of selling untaxed cigarettes. He was placed in a chokehold and died on July 17, 2014, from the result of pressure to his neck and chest.

11. On July 6, 2016, officer Jeronimo Yanez, in Minnesota, shot Philando Castile after a traffic stop.

12. The death of George Floyd occurred on May 25, 2020, in Minneapolis, Minnesota. Police were called after an accusation that Floyd tried to use a counterfeit twenty-dollar bill. During the arrest, a white officer Derek Chauvin knelt on his neck for eight minutes and forty-six seconds, killing him.

13. According to the Black Lives Matter website, the life expectancy of a Black transgender woman is thirty-five years old.

14. Example of this is the Orlando massacre, which generated lots of media coverage.

15. See the site http://www.bullypolice.org/ma_law.html

Chapter 2

Intersections of Race, Gender Identity, and Class of Hate Crimes

> Intersectional identities are not taken into account when it comes to reports of violence. The amount of stories I know in the LGBT community about African American trans, lesbian, gay people who have been murdered in daylight, cold blood, in front of people, that are not headlines is shocking to me.
>
> (Interview with Marta Cunningham,
> Director of Valentine Road)

Scholars of queer studies have critiqued the single identity focus of hate crimes against LGBT communities (Meyer 2008, 2015). In the book *Violence against Queer People: Race, Class, Gender, and the Persistence of Violence*, Doug Meyer argues that gender, race, and class must be taken into consideration when examining hate crimes and violence against LGBT people. Lesbians, especially lesbians of color, experience forms of violence that may differ from gay men of color and transgender women of color (Meyer 23). Black Lives Matter activist Darnell L. Moore during a panel at San Francisco pride with Alicia Garza, Barbara Smith, and Aria Sa'id stated that as a Black gay male he understands that while his life is at risk for violence, he also knows that Black trans women lives are in even more danger than his.[1]

After the Orlando massacre white queer groups and allies paraded signs reading, "We are Orlando." Many queer people of color critiqued the reality that most people in Orlando were queer people of color and experience forms of violence and marginalization that white LGBT people don't (Ramariz et al). Sociologist Salvador Vidal-Ortiz underscored the intersections of violence in the Pulse massacre because the shooter targeted the club on "Latino Night" (Vidal-Ortiz 2016). According to the 2017 National Coalition of Anti-Violence report, 75 percent of LGBT people who experienced hate crimes were people of color with 57 percent being Black.

The intersections of race, citizenship status, class, and gender are relevant in the following cases of high profiled hate crimes in Black and Latinx LGBT communities.

INTERSECTIONS OF RACE, VIOLENCE, AND GENDER IDENTITY: THE CASES OF LATISHA KING, CECE MCDONALD, AND ZORAIDA REYES

On February 13, 2008, fifteen-year-old Latisha King[2] was shot in front of classmates at E.O. Green Junior High School in Oxnard, California. The shooter, fourteen-year-old Brandon McInterney, was offended that Latisha asked him to be his valentine in front of his friends. As a result, Brandon shot Latisha twice in the head in a computer class, where King died from the wounds. Brandon was arrested, and charged with first-degree murder, and hate crime charges. The first trial ended in a hung jury, Brandon was tried a second time, and pleaded guilty to second-degree murder and voluntary manslaughter (Salamon 2018). Various news stories focused on the shooting being a gay-related hate crime, with celebrities, such as Ellen DeGeneres, linking the shooting of Latisha King to gay citizenship (ignoring Latisha's trans identity), arguing that neither she nor Latisha is a second-class citizen (Pringle and Saillant 2008). Similar to the Pulse massacre, white LGBT individuals and groups framed King's death to be only about sexual orientation and/or gender identity—few groups explored the racial and class components to the death.

In the 2013 documentary about the murder entitled, "Valentine Road," Black filmmaker Marta Cunningham, in an interview with Bring Your Own Documentary,[3] discusses the lack of visibility to King murder and lists racism as a possible reason:

> I think that race plays such a huge part in this—I can't even tell you. All this stuff [race, sexuality, class] . . . unfortunately it adds up and then people think, "Oh, well . . . no one is going to buy it. We need someone that we can relate to—we don't relate to this kid." Really, you don't relate to Larry? C'mon. (Cunningham 2013)

Cunningham's statement underscores the challenges of race, capitalism, and sexuality in marketing projects dealing with queer people of color to mainstream audiences. It also illustrates the single-issue politics of hate crimes against LGBT Black and Latinx people; the fact that Latisha King was part

Black and Brandon McInterney was a white supremacist is downplayed, but adds nuances to the crime. The racial makeup of Oxnard is largely Latino/as (73.5 percent), with 48.2 percent white, and 2.9 percent Black (United States Census 2010). Thus, whites are in the minority vis-à-vis Latino/as and racial tensions can exist between the two groups, with whites feeling outnumbered.

Another example of how race played a role in King's murder was media coverage of it. As Cunningham stated, there was a lack of media coverage toward the King murder, which is not unusual when LGBT people of color are killed. The media coverage that appeared framed the murder only as a gay-related hate crime with no discussion of homo/transphobia or white supremacy in or outside E.O. Green Middle School. I interviewed Leticia, a thirty-eight-year-old Latina lesbian from Oxnard about the murder and she remembered working across the street from the school and hearing gunshots:

> I was working in a hospital and we heard gunshots and saw helicopters. We didn't know what happened and it wasn't on the news. I don't remember hearing about it on the news until about two days after it happened. As the case advanced people were more concerned about Brandon, the guy that killed Lawrence not being tried as an adult (prop 21). Many people felt Lawrence was harassing Brandon—that he had this coming to him. There was also a lot of focus on him being in foster care. Like that had anything to do with what happened to him.

Race, gender identity, and class played a role in how little media coverage there was on the Latisha King murder, and how much sympathy there was toward Brandon regarding not being tried as an adult for the murder. As similar hate crime cases against Black and Latinx LGBT communities underscore, victim blaming is pervasive in how the general public views these crimes.

In the book *The Life and Death of Latisha King: A Critical Phenomenology of Transphobia*, Gayle Salamon examines the role of victim blame in a conversation with filmmaker, Marta Cunningham and jurors' decision to declare a mistrial:

> The problem with Larry, they explained, was not that he was gay. They knew Brandon had no problem with Larry's sexual orientation because Brandon had no problem with Marina, another student at E.O. Green, who was gay. When the administrators approached Marina and told her she was not allowed to hold hands with her girlfriend at school, she stopped holding hands with her girlfriend. "Marina got it," said one of the Jurors . . . Larry didn't get it. (Salamon 2018: 151–152)

Salamon is commenting on the desire for the jurors to not see Latisha, and therefore she is labeled as "bad" for wanting to be seen, unlike Marina who knows her place is to be invisible. Latisha was murdered because she dared to be seen, and was viewed as a perpetrator of a crime rather than a victim.

When LGBT Black and Latinx people fight back they are perceived to be the aggressors in a violent situation and disrupt the common narrative that trans people, especially Black trans women, must die when confronted with violence. Just as it is important to document queer Black and Latinx people who have been murdered it is equally important to focus on their survival against both physical and social forms of death. This is the importance of CeCe McDonald's case when focusing on everyday forms of violence and resistance among LGBT Black and Latinx people.

CECE MCDONALD AND THE
DEFENDING OF THE SELF

CeCe McDonald, a Black trans woman, rose to national attention after serving nineteen months of a forty-one-month sentence in prison for confessing to stabbing a man harassing her in self-defense. In June 2011, McDonald and some friends (all were Black) were walking to a grocery store in Minnesota and passed a bar where a group of two white women and a white male were standing outside. After McDonald and her friends passed them, the man, Dean Schmitz, yelled out, "niggers," "faggots," and "chicks with dicks" (Lamont 2012). These slurs show the intersection of identities at play in attacks on Black trans women. The harassment quickly turned violent when Schmitz slashed CeCe's face with a bottle—leaving a scar that required eleven stitches—and chased her as she attempted to leave the scene. In self-defense she stabbed him with a pair of scissors in her purse. She was charged with second-degree murder and in May 2012 accepted a plea bargain for manslaughter.

Similar to the Latisha King case, McDonald experienced character assassination by the media misgendering her. When the jurors were being chosen for her case, it was discovered she had forged a bad check years ago. Meanwhile, Schmitz was seen as an outstanding citizen, not someone with white supremacists ideology out to harm trans and gender nonconforming Black people (Gares 2016).

In addition to pleading guilty to a crime she shouldn't have been convicted for, she was placed in solitary confinement in a men's prison for twenty-three hours a day for four months under the guise of it being for her own protection as a trans woman. In an interview in the *Huffpost* with Marc Lamont, he asked her if she felt in danger in a men's prison. Her response was, "Regardless of if I went to a women's prison or men's prison is fucked up . . . my fear in prison is the same as my fear in the street" (Brekke 2014). McDonald's response highlights the fact that the public sphere of the "free" world is no safer than the privatized incarceration that she and many trans Black and Latinx women experience in jails and prisons. This fact is illustrated in the murders of trans Black and Latinx women who are killed in public spaces, often in front of others. In McDonald's case she was convicted of murder for defending herself, which resembles the case of Marrissa Alexander, who fired a warning shot at her abusive husband. She was convicted of aggravated assault with a deadly weapon where two years before George Zimmerman shot Trayvon Martin using Florida's Stand Your Ground defense.

In both these cases the assailants used the gay and trans panic defense to justify their actions of violence. They also illustrate the intersections of race, gender identity, and class that occur with hate crimes against queer people of color, especially transgender women of color. The following cases are further examples of why sexuality and gender identity are not the only factors in hate crimes against queer Black and Latinx communities.

In Orange County, California Zoraida Reyes, a twenty-eight-year-old Latina transgender woman, was found dead behind a Dairy Queen in June of 2014. Reyes was well-known in queer and immigrant communities fighting for the rights of trans Latinas, especially undocumented queer Latinx people. She was born in Michoacan, Mexico and advocated for trans visibility. She attended Santa Ana Community College, where she received her associate's degree, and later transferred to UC Santa Barbara, but had to drop out because of financial reasons. According to the *Los Angeles Times* (Boster 2014), Reyes body was found outside a fast food restaurant, but police did not rule it foul play or a hate crime (ibid.). However, for the queer community, especially the trans community, foul play must always be considered given the high level of violence in queer and trans communities of color. A few weeks after her murder there was a huge rally in downtown Santa Ana, an area known for its large Latino/a population, that my spouse and I attended, with hundreds of people mourning and protesting the murder, calling for justice to be served.

In October 2014 police arrested a suspect in the murder, thirty-eight-year-old Randy Lee Parkerson, who admitted to choking her during a sexual act. According to Parkerson, he "accidentally" choked her during sex, where she requested to be choked (Emery 2016). He was sentenced to fifteen years to life for second-degree murder. These cases illustrate the intersections of race, class, immigration status, and gender identity, rendering trans women of color illegible subjects to mourn and defend by the general public. Structural barriers to housing, education, and employment also place transgender women of color in danger for physical violence and murder.

King did not have a supportive educational environment, which may have helped protect them from violence; Reyes dropped out of university because of financial challenges, was probably doing sex work at the time of her death (Alokozai 2016), and struggled to obtain stable housing—a reality for many trans women with limited job opportunities. McDonald was once a homeless teen escaping a violent home, and later a prostitute, surviving sexual assault on the streets. All of these trans/gender nonconforming cases illustrate the intersections of various identities and issues society at large devalues.

BLACK LESBIANS AND VIOLENCE

As 2017 came to a close it ended with a high number of Black lesbians (and in some cases their children) murdered. The deaths of these women illumined the intense and often underreported violence against Black lesbians. According to the Huffpost during that time four Black lesbians were murdered in one week (Lohr 2018). On December 28, Kaladaa Crowell was a thirty-six-year-old lesbian who lived in Florida with her eleven-year-old daughter, and partner Robin Denson. Denson's twenty-six-year-old son, Marlin Larice Joseph shot Crowell and her daughter claiming Crowell's daughter had a "bad attitude" (Doris 2018). Crowell was the stepmother of Joseph and there were reports that Joseph was having problems getting along with other children in the house (Lohr 2018).

That same day two women, Shanta Myers, Brandi Mells, and their children, Shanise Myers, five years old and Jeremiah Myers, eleven years old, were murdered in upstate New York. Two men, James White and Justin Mann were indicted. The women's throats were cut and they were found with their feet bound, in spite of the gruesomeness of this murder, it was not deemed a hate crime. Also, that same day on the East Coast, was the murder of twenty-three-year-old Kerrice Lewis in Washington, D.C., who was shot and burned alive in her car. This crime also remains unresolved.

What all these murders have in common are the intersections of race, geography, class, sexuality, and gender identity. In the case of Latisha King the jury used the gay panic defense to justify the murder by a white heterosexual cisgender male (Perkiss 2012). The narrative that King was harassing McInerney reinforces society's fears of hypersexual gay men and trans people, thus providing sympathy for their murders. King was also a person of color from the foster care system, an institution known for creating a pipeline to prison for many queer youth (Gilliam 2004). In other words, the identities King held placed them in deviant categories that the jury viewed as subhuman (i.e., transgender, foster child, non-white).

In the cases of the Black lesbian murders, they share the intersections of class, geography, gender, homophobia, and race in making Black lesbians a target for crime. The murders of Shanta Myers, Brandi Mells happened in

Troy, New York and were described as a robbery. According to the 2012 census Troy, New York has a population of 49,702 and the racial demographics are 71.4 percent white, 16 percent Black, and 9.3 percent Latino/a. Medium income was $39,847. The *Times Union* paper cited Troy and Schenectady as cities with the highest childhood poverty rates in New York state for people of color, with 71 percent Latino/a and 74 percent Black children living below the poverty line (Karlin 2015). The neighborhood that Myers and Mells resided in was a poor/working class city with higher crime rates compared to the rest of the country and New York City (ibid.).

West Palm Beach Florida where Kaladaa Crowell lived has in 2016 a medium income of $41,792 for Blacks, $53,276 for whites, and $34,737 for Latino/as (City-Data.com). This differs significantly from Palm Beach County, which in 2016 had a medium income of $119,843 and was 91.4 percent white, 3.9 percent Latino/a, and 0.5 percent Black (City-Data.com). The neighborhood that Crowell resided in was Progressive Northwest that has a medium income of $24,485, and is 84 percent Black, and 12.2 percent white (Statistical Atlas). The crime rate in West Palm Beach is 95 percent higher than the state, and while unemployment is 3.60 percent (in the state it's 3.80 percent), crime remains a major concern for many residents.[4]

Washington, DC is another place Black lesbians, such as Kerrice Lewis, reside in with a population of 46.4 percent Black, 45.6 percent white, and 11.3 percent Latino/a.[5] The crime rate is concentrated in areas where poverty and drugs are high, those areas being Ward 8. In 2008, hate crimes against LGBT people were at 17.6 percent (Federal Bureau of Investigation Hate Crime Statistics 2008). The area that Lewis lived in, Prince George County, Maryland, also is known for high crimes. This suburb is known for being home to wealthy African Americans, yet like many Black suburbs, crime-ridden areas are not far, and resources are not distributed equally (Lacy 2015). The neighborhood where Lewis' body was found was in Benning Ridge neighborhood, which is surrounded by low-income Blacks even though it is a middle-class neighborhood, where homes sell for $300,000. Lewis like many poor/working class Black lesbians lived with the reality of both structural and community violence. According to the Human Rights Campaign 32 percent of children raised by Black same-sex parents live in poverty, and Black LGBT people are often mistreated by the criminal justice system. Lewis fits this criteria; she had a criminal record and had overcome many struggles associated with being orphaned at a young age. Shanta Myers, Brandi Mells, and Kaladaa Crowell all had children they were raising in working class environments.

Black lesbians are affected by a culture of community violence that marginalizes their identities as queer Black women in Black communities. When analyzing violence against Black lesbians in the form of street harassment,

Heath Fogg Davis argues that "same race street harassment is a behavior pattern, and thus a cultural phenomenon—one that is rooted in black patriarchy" (Fogg-Davis 2006). Hence, the murders of Black lesbians and trans women in Black communities reflect a lack of valuing them as legible community members, and would require a cultural shift in how Black civic society assesses their lives, and hold community members accountable for their well-being. Fogg-Davis urges Black feminists to fight for a cultural shift in behavior among Black people, in addition to analyzing the various intersectional identities of Black women (i.e., class, sexuality, gender identity).

Fogg-Davis takes notes from the 2003 murder of Sakia Gunn in New Jersey, which did not result in mass outrage from the larger Black community, outside of LGBT Black people and allies (Fogg-Davis 2006). Gunn threatened patriarchal expectations when she refused the advances of Richard McCullough who propositioned Sakia and her friends at a bus stop, and later became violent when the girls informed him they were lesbians. McCullough was sentenced to twenty years in prison after a plea bargain was reached dropping charges from murder to aggravated manslaughter, aggravated assault, and bias intimidation (Massey 2005).

Gunn's murder illustrates that both institutional legal violence and homo/transphobia in Black communities are responsible for the violence against Black LGBT people. This recognition calls for creative solutions violence against Black and Latinx LGBT people, such as radical gender socialization beyond male/female binaries in children, LGBT friendly policies in schools, not allowing use of gay/trans panic defenses in the legal system, and the end of homophobia in religious institutions to name a few examples. Since the identities of Black and Latinx individuals are intersecting and complex, so must be the remedies to end violence against them.

CONCLUSION

Everyday violence against Black and Latinx LGBT communities is a result of intersectional oppressions based on race, class, gender, disability, and immigration status. In order to address hate crimes against Black and Latinx communities, one has to examine the root cause of the violence, which stems from institutions such as religion, educational settings, legal system, and families. In addition to these institutions, racial segregation in housing and health care and employment discrimination must also be included. Many queer people of color live in poverty, and are underemployed, thus marginalized in educational settings, placing them on the margins of society. Hence, many live in high-crime areas and/or forced to do sex work—this is especially true of trans Black and Latinx women.

Focusing on hate crimes does not address these underlying issues and assumes a type of subjectivity queer people of color lack (i.e., if it weren't for their sexual orientation/gender identities, they would be full citizens). This reinforces Jasbir Puar's (2007) concept of "homonationalism," which is the normalization of a gay identity (we can extend this to include trans identities), and nationalism. Examples of this are the repeal of don't ask, don't tell in the military, and the legalization of gay marriage—all designed to incorporate queer people into a neoliberal framework of acceptance within U.S. culture. The problem with the framework is that it does not challenge racism, heterosexism, transphobia, classism, xenophobia, or ableism—all of which affect queer people of color. Without a clear integration of these issues within the state and communities of color, violence against queer Black and Latinx people will not decrease, or be addressed properly.

NOTES

1. https://www.youtube.com/watch?v=6NjVvBejXHI

2. I am using the choosing name Latisha to honor the name King went by at the time of the murder.

3. https://filmthreat.com/uncategorized/byod-bring-your-own-doc-episode-110-valentine-road-hbo-documentary-with-director-marta-cunningham/

4. In recent months, there have been a string of murders of Black transgender women (Celine Walker, 36; Antash'a English, 38, and Cathalina Christina James, 24) in Florida, prompting community activist to suspect a serial killer targeting Black trans women (NBC Out, June 2018).

5. https://www.census.gov/quickfacts/DC

Chapter 3

Violence within Families, Institutions, and Communities

When I was transitioning my father shaved my head and told me not to play with dolls, no cooking—all the things I liked to do.

(Interview with Lillian, a Black Caribbean
thirty-three-year-old transgender woman)

In this chapter, I focus on some key themes regarding violence and safety for Black and Latinx LGBT people in and outside of their families, intimate relationships, and communities. Some questions this chapter covers are as follows: How do queer Black and Latinx people view violence within their families? How does anti-LGBT violence interact with other forms of violence, and what is the response from family members to hate crimes against Black and Latinx LGBT members?

VIOLENCE WITHIN FAMILIES

As previously stated, various forms of violence within Black and Latinx families can intersect with queer specific violence. This is particularly the case regarding gender policing of gender roles, and use of violence as a means to maintain gender roles with families. Lillian, a Black Caribbean thirty-three-year-old transgender woman from Florida, now living in Southern California, remembers the connections between her father's domestic violence toward her mother and his policing of her gender:

My father had violent moments. He was physically abusive to my mother and I and really tried to control us.

Male dominance in families is connected to wanting women to obey them, resulting in a strict upholding of gender roles for children deemed to not conforming to them. Family violence does not only mean physical violence. The attack on a person's gender identity and/or sexual orientation can make a Black/Latinx person feel unsafe in their family. Lillian's parents divorced as a result of the physical abuse and her mother remarried. But she remembered verbal remarks from her stepfather that also made her feel unsafe to come out in her family:

> I remember watching TV with my stepfather and if a gay couple was on TV he was say, "Look at them! They are going to burn in hell!" I just thought to myself, "Wow, am I going to burn in hell also?" I was so scared to come out. Growing up Jamaican I would hear in a lot of dance hall music lyrics about killing gay people, killing the battyboy. That scared me. In Jamaican it is still the norm to stone gay people—I didn't want to come out in that environment.

Lillian's comments illustrate that hatred against LGBT people is not only supported on an individual level, but on a cultural one. In the case of Jamaica one area that homophobia is reinforced is in the music, which buttresses homophobia and transphobia within families.

For Black and Latinx people family violence and rejection are common themes, which make them feel unsafe in their families and communities. In addition to individual violence and anti-queer remarks, queer Black and Latinx people experience intimate partner violence and must navigate if they report the abuse to state agencies.

Veronica, a thirty-eight-year-old Black identified queer disabled woman living in Brooklyn experienced intimate partner violence from a Black trans man she was dating, and had to decide whether she would involve the state:

> We had gotten into a heated argument and a physical altercation in the movie theater; someone called the cops. I remember thinking that I wanted to press charges, then I thought, "but what would happen if they check his ID and it says female, what would happen?" Where would they place him? Would they stop helping me? So, by calling police and making an arrest, there is one win, but would it make everything worse in the end? So, I decided not to press charges. I also thought about issues of disability . . . could I get away from this person if I had to? There are many people with invisible disabilities. What counts as having a disability is if you can't defend yourself from violence.

Veronica and Lillian both expressed the impact of being in communities that seem to be indifferent or endorse violence against Black and Latinx LGBT people as a form of everyday violence. Veronica's concerns of further violence by the state (i.e., police) or violence toward her partner at the time caused her to forego getting them involved and handle the situation herself. Intersections of intimate and state violence factor into if queer Latinx and Black people report forms of violence to the police for fear of them not taking the violence seriously or causing more harm. The feeling LGBT Black and Latinx people have of state actors not taking anti-LGBT violence seriously informs encounters with community and family regarding hate crimes.

REACTIONS TO LGBT HATE CRIMES
FROM FAMILY AND COMMUNITY

One of the things that make some Black and Latinx LGBT people feel unsafe among community and family is reactions (or lack of) from family members and community to hate crimes against LGBT people of color. Veronica remembers the silence in the Black community around the 2005 murder of Black gay teen Rashawn Brazell[1]:

> When the murder first happened I remembered people in the community being really upset and invested in finding out what happened to him. As information came out that he was gay it seems I heard less about him and efforts to find him ceased.

When Latisha King was murdered in Oxnard, California, Nancy, a thirty-three-year-old Latina lesbian born and raised in Oxnard, was working across the street at a hospital as a nurse when the shots were fired. Here is what she remembered about the murder and the community response:

> I was working in a hospital a few blocks away, and heard sirens. I thought it was old folks—a fall or something early in the morning. Later I heard gunshots and we saw a helicopter, but never knew what happened. It wasn't until the end of the week that the story came out. What really angered me was that everyone I worked with thought he deserved it. I work with mostly Filipinos and Latinos, so very Catholic upbringing and conservative communities. They go to church, work, and home. That's it. So many people were saying God took him because of the way he was—I felt betrayed. I was like, "Did you forget that I am a lesbian? This was a young person that was murdered in his classroom, and this is what you have to say about this!" I was very scared after that to be around people at work longer than I needed to be.

Veronica and Nancy both expressed the impact of being in communities that seem to be indifferent or endorse violence against Black and Latinx LGBT people as a form of everyday violence. When the Pulse massacre happened myself and other Facebook community members lamented upon the silence from straight activists of color who normally express outrage at police shootings of people of color, but remained silent on the shooting at Pulse nightclub. The lack of social media response from straight activists made many LGBT Black and Latinx people feel unsafe—that they didn't have the support from their straight counterparts toward LGBT issues that they thought.

However, the framing of the shooting as a possible ISIS attack after the identity of the shooter was revealed could also be a possible reason for the silence of some heterosexual activists of color who are otherwise vocal about injustice. The similar co-optation of the case for gun control by some white LGBT activists without analyzing the intersectional components of the case (i.e., racism, xenophobia) is equally frustrating and poses a barrier in fully understanding this attack. Yet, some Black and Latinx LGBT people were deeply hurt at the lack of concern for this attack by friends and family.

Daniel, a gay thirty-two-year-old Latino identified man, was watching the news about the Pulse shooting and felt unsafe around his father after he made disparaging remarks:

> During the news coverage of Pulse my father yelled, "Turn that shit off!" I remember thinking, "But this happened to my community, I could have been there—and this is your reaction."

Neno, a twenty-seven-year-old gender-queer Latinx identified person when remembering Pulse, felt that reactions in their community were not of blatant homophobia, but ambivalence and victim-blaming:

> Some friends of mine were critical of the Islamicphobia of the reporting of the shooting, and others had an attitude of, "Well, that's horrible what happened, but that's what happens when gay people come out." Like, they were suggesting people should stay in the closet.

Tina, a thirty-three-year-old bisexual Haitian American woman from Orange County, California also stated that while straight people in her social circle were horrified about the shooting, there was an undertone of some believing that queer people are responsible for preventing violence from happening to them:

> My straight friends were in shock that the shooting happened at Pulse. When I go out now I am really scared. There is only one gay club I go to and feel safe because I have been going there for years and feel if something happened to me people got my back. My friends will want me to text them when I get to

the club and when I am leaving. They always tell me to be careful. While, I am happy that they care for me and are concerned about my safety, I feel I carry the burden of protecting myself. Not society. Many of us feel there is extra security in our clubs, but not the straight clubs—so the message is that society does not want us to exist.

These statements from queer Black and Latinx people underscore the feeling that the shootings at Pulse nightclub mattered less than other shootings involving people of color and the police. This is what Edelman (2018) speaks of in his article "Why We Forget the Pulse Nightclub Murders: Bodies That (Never) Matter and a Call for Coalitional Models of Queer and Trans Social Justice," lamenting on how quickly the Pulse shooting faded from the political agenda of the mainstream white LGBT movement.

Puar (2007) warned that mainstream white LGBT organizations supported "homonationalism," via queers in the military, adaptation rights, and gay marriage in hopes of creating legible queer bodies that the state would recognize and give citizenship rights to. Hence, the erasure of race and the Islamicphobia by white mainstream gay and lesbian activists regarding the reporting of the shooting.

Nevertheless, the response from some family and community members appears to devalue Black and Latinx queer lives and creates an emotional pain. The responses are a reminder for queer Black and Latinx people that even if individual family members, friends, and/or co-workers appear to accept them—they are still marginalized within those same families and communities. The dearth of anger expressed within some heterosexual and cis-gender Black and Latino/as families and communities extends to race-based social justice movements.[2]

QUEER ERASURE AS VIOLENCE AGAINST BLACK AND LATINX PEOPLE

In spite of organizations, such as Black Youth Project 100 and Black Lives Matter, which formed after the murder of Trayvon Martin, and centers intersectional identities, including gender identity, and sexuality, there exist a false dichotomy of "Blacks" and "Queers." This splitting of these identities underscores the default thinking that queer equals white, and no Black bodies exist in this category. Again, this belief is largely the result of white middle class gay and lesbian people dominating and framing who is a part of the LGBT community, but also the belief among some heterosexual and cisgender Black and brown activists that queer issues are not related to race.[3]

The representation of more queer and trans Black people in the media is a sign of progress and can also distort the level of violence facing the community. Tina comments that she feels many people see queer Black people still at the level of fantasy:

> I feel that while we have more shows on TV featuring Black queer people, many straight people still don't understand our experience and don't see our reality as real.

Sheila Jackson, director of a transgender center in San Francisco, also felt that having more media representation reinforced ideas that trans Black women are entertainment, resulting in their issues not being taken seriously:

> My life is not entertainment; I was a sex worker, not an entertainer. Many Black trans women feel that have to perform as drag queens to gain acceptance. I am funny, but I am not a joke.

Marta Cunningham, commented that what counts as "Black" film contributes to the marginalization of LGBT Black and Latinx stories in Hollywood:

> When I finished Valentine Road, none of the Black film circuits like the Pan African Film festival took it on. It got support from GLADD, Outfest, and Fusion. The message this sends is, "LGBT issues are not Black issues." This is not true . . . racism and homo/transphobia are about people being killed for who they are—especially Black LGBT people. I mean some things are changing, like Moonlight was a great film, but everyone in it except for Janelle Monae was straight. When British Black people play African American characters there is a critique of this . . . there should also be a critique of straight Black actors/actress playing LGBT characters. Where are the Black queer actors?

These statements underscore the need for more than just representation to curb violence against Black and Latinx LGBT people. Particularly, when representation can be used to commodify social movements at the expense of the people who create them.

Dernikos (2016) sheds light on this dilemma in her article "Queering Black Lives Matter," where she focuses on the unintended consequences of public affect regarding people bonding over what seems like a common cause of a movement—in this case around Black people and state violence. She asserts that:

> Although the founders of #BLM have specifically proclaimed that all Black lives matter—"the lives of Black queer folks and trans folks, disabled folks,

Black-undocumented folks, the folks with records, women and all Black lives along the gender spectrum" (#BlackLivesMatter 2015, sec.4)—not every/body seems to be orientated towards the same directive. This raises the question: Which Black lives are we really talking about? (p. 6)

Lillian echoes Dernikos analysis stating that in spite of the queer and feminist foundation of Black Lives Matters, it has been presented as a movement for non-trans, straight Black men's lives to matter:

I think that even though Black women started Black Lives Matter—it's evident that it's only the lives of cisgender straight Black men that matter in many of these Black activists spaces. When Black trans women are murdered we hear nothing from the larger Black community. We need to shame people who murder Black trans women; make it seem like a crime—shame them the way the community shames Black men for dating a trans woman, so we can hold that murder to the same level as we hold Black men who are murdered. Black lives matter—what about us? It's the same with the Me2 movement, which was started by Black women, but we only heard about it by white women in Hollywood. Black people pick and choose who they will support; it's all based on what makes the news. Most Black trans women are killed by Black men—the community doesn't want to deal with that.

Since the creation of Black Lives Matter, many people have appropriated the meaning, disregarding the leadership, and turned it against the very Black and Latinx queer and trans people it was meant to protect. This is evident when I teach about Black Lives Matter in my Introduction to African American Studies course, when often students, especially Black men, are shocked when they learn the movement was started by three Black women, two being queer identified. This information disrupts the heteronormative masculine narratives of Black social movements.[4]

Yet, one cannot underestimate the patriarchal heteronormative focus of white owned media outlets, which highlight the deaths of Black heterosexual non-trans identified men over trans/queer Black women and Black LGBT people. According to Ritchie (2015), police violence against Black women and LGBT people does not make into the media coverage, since most stories focus on straight non-trans Black men. The focus on mainstream media is important here because the degree of trans and LGBT support within the various chapters of Black Lives Matter is distorted via images of only cisgender straight Black men as racial subjects of state violence. For example, a few months after the police shooting of Mike Brown in Ferguson, Tanisha Anderson was killed in Cleveland, Ohio. However, unlike Brown's case it did not spark a national movement (Ritchie 2015). Hence, the media helps to create the narrative that Black LGBT lives matter less within the movement, in spite of its queer leadership.

EVERYDAY VIOLENCE AND INTERSECTIONS

For queer Black and Latinx people everyday violence can take on many forms that are not only limited to "gay bashings," which often assumes that queerness is the only identity that makes queer people targets for violence (Meyer 2015). Public safety is a concern for many trans and gender nonconforming people of color, especially coming home at night on public transportation, or catching a taxi or Uber in the daytime. Nena describes an uncomfortable experience she and her girlfriend had in an Uber in San Francisco going to Oakland:

> A few times when my girlfriend and I were in an Uber in San Francisco going to Oakland, and we get in the car and the Uber driver starts making comments about how he likes lesbians, but thinks gay men are gross. He started asking us what we do in bed. The whole ride was really uncomfortable. A few weeks ago on the bus, a fight broke out, with someone was threatening to shoot this gay couple. Luckily, no one was seriously injured and people stopped the fight.

The fear of being out in public spaces for queer people, especially trans and cisgender women of color, has been well documented (Doroshwalther 2014; Meyer 2015). The criminal justice system instead of protecting queer people of color from violence promotes state violence via criminalizing queer people of color for defending themselves against an attack (Doroshwalther 2014).

Veronica remembers when she and her partner a Black trans man were on the bus and gay bashed:

> We were on the bus and I leaned my head on his shoulder . . . two guys (one Black, one Latino) looked at him and said something about someone acting like a man. At that point some people got off, some were just watching. The guys starting walking towards back where we were sitting; some people jumped in to help, they were mostly white. It was really scary. Eventually, they got off the bus, but I wasn't sure what was going to happen. Now I am currently dating a femme woman, who can pass as straight. I am still scared of being gay bashed. Once a group of Afro-Latino boys walked towards us and we wondered if we should stop holding hands, but didn't want to. They walked around us, and I heard them talking, "That's funny because they don't look gay." They too pretty to be dykes." We were read as physically attractive to them—it made us safe, but we felt really sad.

In addition to being queer other marginal identities can make queer Black and Latinx individuals targets for violence inside and outside of queer spaces. For instance, Nena remembers being in Virginia during her teens and having white neighbors yell anti-immigrant statements to her:

> I remember people saying, "Go back to your own country." I didn't have a green card, and I was such an overachiever in high school, not waiting to draw attention to myself, or make other immigrants look bad.

Violence docs not only happen in straight spaces for queer Black and Latinx people, but also in white queer spaces. Nena remembered going to a queer party in San Francisco and being harassed:

> My girlfriend and I went to a queer party in San Francisco, which turned out to be mostly white. People were touching us and trying to get us to dance together. It was really weird and I couldn't wait to get out of there.

Anti-Black/Latinx behavior can be pervasive in white queer spaces from the racist performance of drag queen Shirley Q. Liquor who portrays a Black Southern welfare mother, to the criminalization of Black and Latinx patrons at white gay establishments requiring multiple forms of identification. At the Toronto Pride 2016 Black Lives Matter staged a protest in response to anti-Black racism within the white queer community (Greey 2018). These events reinforce the need for Black and Latinx LGBT spaces that affirm the intersections of their identities. It is important to also point out that violence is often intraracial, meaning violence happens within similar ethnic groups, and is not unique to one particular group.

A few Black women I spoke with stated that they feel unsafe in straight Black spaces, especially around some cisgender Black men. Tina felt unsafe around straight Black men citing a feeling of not knowing when the vibe will change with them:

> When I am in Black straight spaces, I feel most unsafe with straight Black men—not all, but some. I feel safe up until a certain point, then I feel some men will want to hit on me or might do something to me thinking they can change me.

Lillian also felt unsafe around most cisgender straight Black men citing their need to keep the fact that many of them date trans women a secret as a source of violence:

> Many Black straight cisgender men are on the DL (down-low), when it comes to dating and being attracted to trans women. I fear what would happened if I

am outed in certain spaces. There is a pecking order when it comes to whose
Black lives matter: Cisgender Black men, then cisgender Black women, Black
gay men, Black lesbians, Black trans men, and Black trans women at the bottom—especially the ones without passing privilege.

These statements address the fear of violence for Black and brown queer
people that exist within and outside of ones' community. This is an important
point because addressing and ending violence against Black and Latinx queer
communities requires an intersectional approach, and can't be narrowed
down to one cause responsible for the violence. In white queer spaces, race
may make someone a target for harassment, while in straight people of color
spaces, gender identity and/or sexual orientation does. The issue of economic
class and access to resources is instrumental to how queer Black and Latinx
people experience violence.

INSTITUTIONAL VIOLENCE

Violence against queer Black and Latinx people does not have to be physical, but often institutionalized within educational, religious, and employment
settings. The concept of economic violence first came into existence via the
feminist movement of the 1960s and 1970s to address oppression of women
in heterosexual relationships with men who withhold financial information,
access to credit, and checking accounts. It was later used to describe the relationship between the state and women of color on welfare as a form of state
violence (Nadasen 2005; Bridges 2011). For queer Black and Latinx people
economic violence is connected to family and state institutions. This is evident in the marginal status of queer Black and Latinx individuals in employment, legal, religions, and educational settings (Mogul, Ritchie, and Whitlock
2011; Moore 2015). Queer Black and Latinx people experience institutional
violence often in educational and religious settings.

Lillian remembers her early experiences moving from New York to Florida
and going to church as a young trans woman and how that connected with her
educational experiences:

I grew up in New York City and was surrounded by Black and Latino kids in
school until middle school. When I was thirteen I moved to Florida to live with
my grandparents during my middle and high school years. They lived in Haines
city, which was very white and conservative. I had forced Bible study and the
church they went to was 80% white. It was hard being queer, all you heard
was how it was a sin. I was also bullied in school for being queer, to a point
that I was homeschooled my last year of middle school. I went to a public high

school, which had more people of color, and my grandparents had this attitude of, "Don't let what happened at the old school happen here." They felt I was an embarrassment to the community they were trying to be a part of.

Lillian's experiences highlight the victim-blaming by family and community when queer violence happens against Black and Latinx individuals, especially those adhering to respectability politics. Universities can be a site of violence toward queer Black and Latinx students. Veronica remembers her experiences at a university on the East Coast with trying to establish both Black and queer student spaces and the resistance she got.

> This university consisted of far right straight white kids, queer white groups and Black groups where sexism and homophobia were common. I made myself visible, running for positions; I started getting calls in my dorm. In my sophomore year I got a call from drunk guy asking me "Where did you get those sheets on your bed?" He proceeded in describing what I was wearing, my room. It was really scary. I fell into a depression. Shortly, after I started to receive death threats. I got some support from white queer people and queer black support, but from other Blacks it was 50/50.

For queer college students of color, they must fit into preexisting identity-based groups that don't fully include them (i.e., Black Student Union groups, or white queer groups), or form their own institutions, which are often met with administrative pushback.

Concerning religion, Veronica also received homophobic messaging in church and this was reinforced by her grandmother's views toward her sexuality:

> My grandparents who taught me to stand up for what I believed in adopted me. My grandmother supported about everything about me, but my queerness. She viewed it as a sin and a choice. I came out in college in the 90s; my grandmother loved me but wish that wasn't there . . . but she recognized my character was good, I didn't turn into an asshole (laughs). So, maybe being queer wasn't that bad. Later she supported my relationships. She loved me, but still said homophobic things based on the churches she was involved in. If something happened regarding laws and LGBT rights, or if something happened to me because I was queer, I didn't know what her response would be. She offered conditional support—she thought, "That is a risk you take for being gay. Done in the name of Jesus."

Many queer people of color come from religious families where they were given contradictory messages about their acceptance within their family.

Similar to the "Don't Ask, Don't Tell" policy in the military, some Black and Latinx LGBT people are accepted within families as long as they don't bring evidence of being queer to them. For example, not bringing partners over, or discussing queer issues.

This struggle for acceptance extends past families and communities and into the workforce. Lillian remembers her struggles trying to obtain employment while she was transitioning:

> My first job was at Legoland, until my supervisor outed me because my legal documents weren't changed so I could work as a woman. I also wasn't sure what would happen if I showed up as female with a male gender. I applied for a job at McDonalds, but the manager ignored my application. My ID photo was not feminine enough even though I had on a wig. I didn't have a lot of girl clothes and I didn't have a car. I was educated, but couldn't get a job at McDonalds. I later got a job at Verizon, but they said in order for me to work, I had to work as a male, since that is what it said on my ID. I did sex work to survive until I got a job as a fine arts assistant in college.

Lillian's experiences with transphobia in the workplace are a common form of institutional violence trans and gender nonconforming Black and Latinx people face. In relation to hate crimes, it is important to understand that by the state denying queer people of color jobs, health, education, and housing, the state creates a context for hate crimes to occur.

Polices that marginalize Black and Latinx people within these institutions make them targets for hate crimes because by the state withholding these services, it gives permission for ordinary individuals to deny life, liberty, and justice in the form of institutional hate crimes against this group.

CONCLUSION

In this chapter, I explored violence within families and communities of Black and Latinx people, and the intersections of institutional violence. Black and Latinx queer people experience violence in places where they are supposed to feel safe: within their families and racial communities. The violence many Black and Latinx LGBT people face in their families is connected to male violence and patriarchy within the home, where patterns of violence and conflict over gender roles between parents are already established—creating an unsafe environment for queer children.

This marginalization is reinforced in educational, legal, and religious settings, which pushes many queer people of color into precarious economic situations, where they may experience violence. This chapter expands what is meant by violence and hate crimes via underscoring that the everyday homophobia and transphobia queer Black and Latinx people face within families and institutions are extended forms of hate crimes—from apathy when queer people of color are murdered, to religious hatred queer Black and Latinx people experience in church, to harassment in schools, universities, and employment. Until these forms of violence and marginalization are addressed within institutional settings, conversations and solutions about hate crimes that occur in families or on the street will be inadequate.

NOTES

1. Rashaw Brazell was a nineteen-year-old gay Black male who was murdered and dismembered in Brooklyn, New York in 2005. In 2017, Kwauhuru Govan, one of Brazell's former neighbors was arrested.

2. This was evident during the uprising after the police murder of George Floyd. Oluwatoyin Salau, a young Black woman and Black Lives Matter activist, was found dead in Florida after being raped and assaulted.

3. After the Pulse shooting while speaking to some Black heterosexual academic friends, I was surprised that many thought the victims were white prior to seeing photos of them because they were queer and the shooting happened at a "gay" club.

4. Another hopeful indicator that Black Queer lives are being valued is the march that occurred in front of the Brooklyn Museum on June 14, 2020.

Chapter 4

Family and Community
Impact of Violence

Before Gwen's murder my life was great. I had a wonderful job as paralegal, I had a good relationship with my family; I was dating. Now I am homeless and I haven't had an income since 2002. Most of my family members have turned their backs on me thinking I should be over it by now. They don't understand PTSD.

(Interview with Sylvia Guerrero, mother
of slain trans teen Gwen Araujo)

The community impact of LGBT-related violence and hate crimes has been well researched with studies documenting the effect of Matthew Shepard's murder upon LGBT individuals (Bell and Perry 2015). However, there is little research on the family impact of LGBT-related violence upon parents, surviving siblings, and neighborhood community members of color. There is less research on differences within anti-LGBT violence (Walters et al. 2017), especially in communities of color. In this chapter, I highlight challenges faced by survivors of hate crimes, and family members of murdered loved ones.

One of the hate crime cases that brought attention to violence against LGBT Black women was the death of Sakia Gunn. In 2003, Sakia Gunn, a fifteen-year-old Black lesbian from Newark, New Jersey, was coming home from Greenwich Village waiting for a bus with her friends, when two men made sexual advances toward them, and one stabbed Sakia, after she refused their advances (Fogg-Davis 2006). While the murder of Sakia Gunn did not generate the same media attention and public outage as Matthew Shepard's, it emphasized the dangers for Black LGBT youth. Gunn's murder

48 Chapter 4

also underscores one of the challenges facing hate crimes against Black and Latinx people—lack of media attention or racist media coverage.

In Newark, California, four men murdered seventeen-year-old Gwen Arajuo at a party over the course of three hours after being outed as trans. According to Gwen's mother, Sylvia Guerrero, when Gwen went missing, the media wanted to report her as a runaway, instead of a missing teen:

> When Gwen first went missing, and we filed a police report, they put down that she was a runaway. They concluded because she was Latina and in their minds lived in a bad neighborhood, that she must be a runaway. I found that very offensive and it illustrated the disregard that they had for her.

In addition to disrespectful assumptions by police, Gwen was misgendered, like many trans people in the media, and teachers in Gwen's school blamed Sylvia for her murder:

> I saw what transphobia did to Gwen. She was a happy child, but over time she became angry from bullying throughout her childhood. Schools didn't know me; I was viewed as an angry mother—they didn't see the loving mom I was. Teachers blamed Gwen for things she didn't do—like use the boy's bathroom. She never went to high school, but continuation school. I pulled her out of school because boys gave her a hard time for using the girl's bathroom.

Similar to the murder of Latisha King, trans teens of color are blamed for their deaths by not conforming to the gender binary system, along with parents who are supportive of their children's gender identity. This victim blaming can also lead families experiencing hate crimes to feel isolated, both outside and within their communities and families.

ISOLATION WITHIN FAMILIES AND COMMUNITIES

Many families of color experience forms of isolation after the hate crime of a loved one. After the murder of Gwen, Sylvia started to experience isolation from within her family and her larger community:

> When the murder first happened, I had a lot of support from family and the larger LGBT community. It was hard to accept awards and be on television . . . sometimes I couldn't be that strong, but people understood. Every mother's day I would get people donating to our fund, but now—nothing. For eight years I got support, especially when the story was hot in the media, and everyone wanted to interview me. Even people in my own family feel I should be over

this. My relationships with my other children have deteriorated over the years. We lived in a rural town in Newark, California—very backwards. When Gwen was murdered the Portuguese community donated food for the funeral, but in general the white community was very conservative at the funeral. The church we went to disowned Gwen once she started transitioning, so we stopped attending. When Gwen was killed, not one church member came to door to reach out and help.

The isolation Sylvia describes reflects the type of marginalization experienced by LGBT Black and Latinx people within their families and communities—the kind of isolation that leads to hate crimes happening in the first place. It also illustrates how Black and Latinx families affected by hate crimes are marginalized vis-à-vis their white counterparts, especially when it comes to economic support. Sylvia compares her situation to that of Matthew Shepard's mother, Judy Shepard:

Ironically, Gwen and I talked about the murder of Matthew Shepherd when it happened. After Gwen's death I worked with the Horizon Foundation, which worked to establish Gay Straight Alliances (GSA) in the high schools. The foundation also did a Gwen Araujo Transgender Education fund. We worked with 73 schools; Horizon paid $500 and the GSA got $500. Kids loved it. Eventually, people stopped donating; we did Montel Williams and Tyra Banks shows. People aired the Horizon number for people to donate; the second ad to be aired was the Transgender Education Fund, but they didn't show the name Gwen Araujo. They claimed there is only $200 in the fund. They looked over records and claimed $200 was dominated. I believe it was more. We got $150 from the Tyra Banks Show—it shows you how people didn't care about transgender issues in 2007. They didn't charge it as hate crime. Meanwhile, Judy Shepherd's fund is thriving; she came from a wealthy family. Matt's mother had more support—more media attention. Gwen can't be as big as Matthew Shepherd. I reached out to the GLADD organization; they denied helping, never returned my calls. But they gave awards for the lifetime movie based on Gwen's story.[1] In my GoFundMe fund there was $11,000 in three in half years—I can't live on that for 3 years.

Sylvia expresses the economic disparity not only in the lives of transgender Black and Latinx people, but also in death. The fact that Gwen's fund does not have consistent donations compared to the continual media coverage, and publishing opportunities for Judy Shepard surrounding the murder of Matthew Shepard is telling in its exposure of transphobia and racism. It also speaks to the financial precarity surrounding the families of Black and Latinx communities, which is underscored in the event of a murder or assault.

The financial challenges upon loved ones of a murdered victim via hate crimes are compounded by anti-LGBT biases regarding finding burial grounds and religious members of a community to conduct a service. This was what happened with the service of Zoraida Reyes on the day of her funeral according to one of her good friends Javier, who planned most of the service:

> When we were trying to find a Catholic Church to hold the service, many refused us. They wouldn't hold service or bury her because she was transgender and that went against their religious beliefs. Even her mother couldn't get them to change their minds, so we finally found a Catholic Church and it was $100 more than the other churches. Overall, the service was about $13,000 most of which was raised by a GoFundMe account through different organizations and people in the community. So, her family didn't have to pay anything.

This situation shows that stigma is not limited to an individual person but extends to their family and community resulting in shame and has financial implications. Ramona Sanchez, fifty-two-year-old queer identified Latinx woman who works with the nonprofit organization, Pulse One, expressed how stigma and financial hardship affected the survivors and victims of the Pulse massacre:

> I feel if the victims were white there would be more people providing housing, money. Some people got kicked out of their apartments once it was discovered they were gay. Some couldn't return to work because of PTSD. Many didn't tell their parents—especially gay Latin men because of the Catholic religion. I see survivors who want to let people know they can do speaking engagements—it's like, "What can I get out of it?" Some tried to continue on with work; one survivor graduated from the United Airlines; some want to continue going to events at a gay bar, or bartend in one. I just feel if they were white and straight more doors would open—like housing. I worked with an organization that has 166 units of affordable housing for the survivors, but the apartments are in drug-fested areas. Also, some churches would host some of the victims' funerals. This was the case with performer Shane Tomlinson, his family had a hard time finding a church to give him a service. The Greenwood Cemetery provided space for four of the Pulse victims to be buried. They are also going to have a memorial dedicated to the victims.

In addition to trauma from having a loved one murdered, Black and Latino/a parents have to contend with discrimination and anti-LGBT sentiments even when trying to bury their loved ones (Ogles 2017). Parents of a child who experienced a hate crime may also be isolated within their larger family, as was the case with Sylvia. However, isolation after a hate crime does not only occur among family and community, but also within the workplace.

WORKPLACE VIOLENCE AND HATE CRIMES

P. Rodriguez, a trans identified Afro-Latinx person, was the first director of diversity, equity, and inclusion at Philadelphia's Unity Center,[2] which is a health care provider for queer people. P. was recently fired by the agency in what has become a controversy within the LGBT community in Philadelphia. They also experienced two hate crimes, the first of which happened while working at the Unity Center, and they didn't receive any support from the CEO:

> The first time I experienced a hate crime was when I was working at the Unity Center at the Transgender Wellness Conference. While we were there providing information to the trans community, there was a right-wing Christian group protesting us. They were yelling, "homosexuals going to hell!" "God hates trans." They were saying targeted things to people. I told the CEO that our organization was not prepared to deal with this—my comments were disregarded. There was no structure; everyone did their own thing. We confronted them, and told them that they will leave and not take up space. A man of color who had the microphone punched me in the face; I had a cut on my nose. A white colleague saw the whole thing; we called the police and they took forever to come. When they did nothing was done about the situation. Later the CEO told me that I should have walked away from the situation, that I reacted in a non-professional manner.

The lack of action by police and employers in responding to the hate crime P. experienced underscores how trans/non-confirming people are blamed for evoking violence toward themselves. The police view queer Black and Latinx people as instigators of violence instead of being the ones needing protection. P.'s workplace, especially being a health clinic that serves LGBT clients, should have had trained professionals to handle hate crime-related violence on the job (similar to threat of violence or actual violence against abortion providers), but instead there wasn't any infrastructure to address the issue.

An employed person, who experiences a hate crime and needs medical attention, can seek treatment via their health insurance that hopefully will cover a portion of medical expenses. However, when someone is unemployed and/or without health insurance, the care they seek can be minimal. The second hate crime P. experienced occurred after they were fired from the Unity Center and no longer had health insurance. They were at a concert in

New York in a large crowd, when a white cisgender male punched them in the face:

> I was at Terminal 5 concert hall in New York it was a LGBT concert, but the space was white and straight. My friend, a white trans man, and I had been drinking, so I was not sober. We were close to the stage, so people push into each other. A white lesbian couple were to my left, and I bumped into them; a masculine person pushed me back. A Black older man security guard was eyeing me, targeting me—the only trans person of color there. A white man was in front of me with a woman, they got into it protecting the white lesbian . . . he asked, "Are you a boy/or a girl?" Before I could respond he punched me in eye and mouth. My friend broke up fight not security—actually I continued getting misgendered by security guards. I filed a police report. I was unemployed and uninsured; I had to advocate for myself, which meant refusing cost. I took Uber to hospital; I got 1 butterfly stickers instead of stitches. Basically, I had prioritized the cost and not my care. Luckily, I put up some photos of my injuries on a GoFundMe page and already raised $7,500. The Internet has been a great resource for trans people of color to share stories and get resources.

P.'s experience speaks to the intersections of transphobia, race, and class when accessing resources from surviving a hate crime. When they were working, and had health insurance, they were viewed as being unprofessional in how they handled the first situation of violence, and was ultimately fired, leading them to be in a fragile financial position when experiencing the second hate crime. Furthermore, the failure again of the state (in the form of a security guard) in stopping violence against LGBT Black and Latinx people is underscored in this example. The security guard was actually protecting the people harassing P.

Bamby Salcedo, president and CEO of the Trans Latin@ Coalition, which serves the needs of the trans Latina community in Los Angeles, spoke about the economic challenges of hate crimes on the transgender community:

> If someone experiences a hate crime they could lose their job because sometimes a person may need to take time from work for medical and legal reasons, and employers may not be sensitive to that, also people may not have health insurance. All of these effect how a hate crime will affect them.

Both Bamby and P. discussed the role of the workplace in facilitating a safe space where LGBT employees feel safe and are supported in the unfortunate event of a hate crime. They also speak to the narrative of Black and Latinx LGBT people being constructed as "unprofessional" in the workplace, rather it's how they handle hate crimes against them by fighting back, or lack of resources available to them (i.e., not taking off work to file complaints) that render them undeserving of support.

Workplace violence can happen among community members. This occurred when I went to interview Bamby for this project at TransLatina Collation in Los Angeles. While in her office we heard some commotion outside in the hallway, it was during lunchtime, so people were having lunch in the common area. Suddenly, we heard screaming and things being thrown on the floor. Bamby rushed out of the office down the hall; I looked to see a Black trans woman being punched in the face, and her hair being pulled by a Latinx trans woman. The fight was broken up and the Black trans woman was led into an empty office to calm down. I gathered that the women knew each other and may have been fighting over a guy. The Black trans woman was homeless living on Skid Row and was worried about her hair being messed up since she went to great lengths to have her hair done. She had scars on her face and her shorts revealed scars on her thighs.

For trans women and other members of color in the LGBT community, violence is both external and internal—it comes from the state, strangers on the street, family, and within the LGBT community. This is important when understanding everyday violence; that the marginalization from lack of housing, jobs, and health care places many trans women of color in dangerous circumstances. These issues sometimes bleed into the spaces that are supposed to be safe. However, unlike the above experience with P. Bamby, other community members were able to end the fight without relying on the police, who would have made the situation worst. This is an example of community accountability and alternatives to calling the police when intra-community violence occurs. It also speaks to the issue of structural violence, and the challenges of creating safe spaces for trans women of color. Hate crimes and violence in general are problems for many poor working class transgender Black and Latinx women, along with PTSD (Reisner 2016).

CONCLUSION

In this chapter I analyzed the community and family impact of hate crimes against LGBT Black and Latinx people. Families and survivors of anti-LGBT-related hate crimes experience family isolation, financial hardship, and community stigma. This stigma is evident in difficulties of families finding a church service for their murdered loved one, lack of intervention against preventing violence, and victim blaming of those who survived hate crimes, especially transgender people of color.

This isolation speaks to the limits of community for many queer Black and Latinx people and their families—it highlights the continued work of families, religious institutions, and workplaces to create safe and affirming environments for LGBT Black and Latinx people. Religious institutions must be open to honoring the gender identity of transgender people and their families wishes for religious services at their funerals, not turning these families away or charging them extra money to perform a service. Families should support loved ones who have experience hate crimes by providing emotional and at times financial support—not avoiding what happened because of anti-LGBT stigma from neighbors or other community members.

Lastly, workplace culture needs to be more informed about LGBT issues beyond HR departments honoring same-sex marriage benefits. This is very important in light of the recent Supreme Court decision, which ruled that VII protects LGBT workers. Workplaces need to be informed about violence in the workplace against LGBT individuals, and legal resources need to be utilized to protect LGBT employees from violence. These steps can help eradicate the isolation many LGBT people of color feel when a hate crime has occurred, and improve the mental health of those in emotional distress.

NOTES

1. Holland, A. 2006. *A Girl Like Me: The Gwen Araujo Story. Lifetime.*
2. Name of this business is changed to a pseudonym.

Chapter 5

Impact of Violence on Mental Health and Activism

Before the Pulse shooting my boyfriend and I would go to gay clubs all the time. Now he doesn't want to go out as much, especially to a gay club.

(Interview with Angel, 25
Pulse Shooting survivor)

After the Pulse shooting, many people I knew in the Black/Latinx LGBT community were scared to attend pride events; others became more determined to be out in the LGBT community and increased their activism. Natasha Robinson, a twenty-three-year-old trans Black/Latinx woman, who works at the #One Pulse Foundation, stated that the Pulse tragedy really shook people's sense of safety, including her own:

I woke up in the middle of the night and learned what happened on Facebook. I was in shock. Pulse was a safe place. There were only three queer clubs, but Pulse was more than a gay club nightclub. Parents would come, straight people—everyone there. We often judge each other, including in the LGBT community. The rest of the LGBT community judges trans people. But at Pulse I never worried about being judged. After the shooting that safe place was taken away. You are left thinking, "Where do I fit in the world?" I was ten years old when 9/11 happened-I didn't really remember it. But I remembered this.

For many queer people of color, Pulse highlighted our worse fears of what can happen to Black and Latinx LGBT people—that we will be murdered. The theme and the fear of violence is what keeps many queer people of color in the closet and it is often the first thought of friends and family members when someone comes out as queer and/or transgender—that violence will happen to them. Hate crimes have a lasting impact on survivors and the surrounding community. This is evident in Sylvia's interview where she continues to experience PTSD seventeen years after the murder of her transgender daughter, Gwen Araujo, and viewing photos of her daughter's body worsened her PTSD:

> In retrospect I should not have looked at the autopsy photos . . . that was a mistake. I remember I couldn't get the images of her beaten and mutilated body out of my head. I still close my eyes and see those images and have flashbacks of being in court with those photos up there during the trial.

Sylvia continues to be traumatized by these images, even as they were helpful during the trial. PTSD is common for LGBT Black and Latinx who experienced hate crimes, and often they have not received therapy. Racquel Sanchez, a fifty-two-year-old worker at the Pulse One Foundation, has yet to receive therapy after the massacre, even as she helps others get mental health treatment:

> I still have a problem on June 12th going to Pulse; part of the task force is to go every month for the memorial. At 7am I am there interviewing other people on their thoughts regarding the memorial. The help is there, counseling is there—as a community we have done an amazing job. I have yet to get therapy.

Many survivors of hate crimes feel abandoned by their ethnic communities. This was the case with Grant, a forty-five-year-old Black gay-identified man living in Southern California who was attacked when he was twenty-four years old in Oakland, California, outside of some housing projects:

> My brother, some friends, and I were outside of these housing projects in Oakland, and a group of Black boys ran outside with bats and chains, yelling anti-gay things. My brother and friends ran away but they jumped me and I had a busted face, broken ribs. I didn't have health insurance, so I didn't go to the hospital. Never got any therapy. That attack had a profound effect on me. I felt like Black people didn't care about me, or that Black men, might attack me for no reason. It's crazy. I feel some Black men try to judge me and see if I'm gay or a threat to them in any way.

Fear is a common outcome for survivors of hate crimes; many fear going into queer spaces; others fear being seen with a partner that is gender nonconforming in public because of risk of violence and being visually outed as queer.

This is what Veronica, who survived a hate crime that happened to she and her partner on a bus in New York City experienced:

> I still felt fairly safe by myself. I'm what most people would consider pretty damned effeminate in dress and mannerism, etc. So if a strange man came up to me, it was more likely that he was there to hit on me than physically hit me for being perceived as gay. But when I was on a date . . . or with friends who presented as more masculine, as less gender-normative . . . those moments were always filled with a little fear. I'm the kinda person who doesn't like to be forcibly silenced. All that will do is make me even more determined to speak up. So in some ways that experience made me even more bold about being out.

Nia, a thirty-eight-year-old Black feminine presenting lesbian also felt fearful when with masculine presenting women of possible violence:

> When I am with my straight women or femme lesbian friends and I am linked arm and arm with them in public, I don't fear being attacked, but if I am with a masculine partner, I do have that fear in the back of my mind. Also, I have a chronic illness, so if I am on the subway and see some guy being called a "faggot," I think about if I am going to jump in and help him because I am thinking about my own safety.

In addition to fear, some people spoke about the feeling of wanting to be more out after experiencing or hearing about a hate crime. When Zoraida Reyes was murdered many LGBT Latinx people, especially trans women, felt a need to become more involved in activism. Tony, a gay-identified Latino cisgender male who works at the LGBT center in Orange County:

> When Zoraida was murdered everyone just sorta woke up and became more active. This was especially true of the trans Latinx women here in Orange County. We always knew about hate crimes, but it's different when it happens in your own community . . . it's more real.

While some were inspired to become better activists, others engage in distancing from LGBT communities and/or victim blaming (Bell and Perry 2015). For example, when I was talking with Tony he stated that while Zoradia's death lit a fire under some community members to be more involved in the LGBT community, some trans Latinx women viewed Zoradia's death as a product of her naivety, with what some people in the community concluded, her participation in sex work:

> Some of the trans women kind of blamed her for the murder, like she didn't know what she was doing. They had the attitude like that wouldn't happen to them because they were smarter than that.

Dissociation is a response of many marginalized populations upon hearing news that a loved one has been murdered, and a way of easing fears that it may happen to them. An example of this dissociation is the organizing of an "ex-gay freedom march" by two survivors of the massacre, Angel Colon and Luis Javier Ruiz, who claim to be no longer gay.[1]

Some participants were affected by hate crimes in their dating and personal lives. Lillian, a Black trans woman, expressed that hate crimes impacted her mental health when it came to dating and meeting new people:

> Hearing about hate crimes has really affected my attitude towards dating and meeting new people. Based on past experiences of violence, I fear dating and putting myself out there in social settings.

While some people limited their physical space, Nia described reducing the time she spends on Facebook and other social media to take care of her mental health:

> If I go on Facebook I limited my time on it because you always see something about a hate crime, especially against trans women of color. It's depressing, and in our political climate I feel we are hearing more about these types of things happening. Like in New York a man attacked these Black lesbians on the subway, paralyzing one of them. It's scary . . . sometimes you just need a break from the media.

Self-care is important for Black and Latinx queer people who consistently hear about murders in our communities. Some people take care of their mental health by gathering with others at memorial services for fallen loved ones. While gathering can provide solace for some people who attend these rallies, it can also provoke anger when comparing the size of the crowd for queer people of color versus cisgender men of color. Nia made the following observation upon attending a gathering for violence against Black women in New York:

> This was during a time when there were murders of both trans and cisgender Black women. I was at the rally and found myself getting angry because it was a small crowd. To make matters worse, there were a group of Black men playing soccer near by and the ball was accidentally kicked into the crowd . . . so these men saw the crowd and didn't care about the lives of Black women. Also, a few years ago a Black gay man was murdered in the West Village and I went to place flowers down on the spot he was killed. I was angry that this was not a march in NYC the way it would have been if the police killed a Black straight cisman.

Hence, memorials can both honor LGBT Black and Latinx people murdered by hate crimes and underscore the marginalization of these groups at the same time. Chas Brack, the producer and director of the documentary, "Dreams Deferred: The Sakia Gunn Project," stated that the project came about because the LGBT community in Newark, New Jersey needed it:

> The murder of Sakia Gunn didn't get the attention as Matthew Shepherd's did and the community knew her story needed to be told. We have learned as LGBT Black people that nobody is going to tell our stories but us, so we have a respon sibility to tell stories of marginalized people of color.

Hate crimes can mobilize queer Black and Latinx communities into action. Bamby Salcedo discussed this aspect of empowerment when describing the services provided at TransLatin@ Coalition:

> When trans women of color have traumatic experiences, they don't have the visibility and resources to attend to their mental health. People who may have work, you have to miss work . . . to seek support you need . . . police, hospital, court. Do you have to relocate?

> They may not be able to afford it. Hate crimes happened to the most disad-vantaged: women, immigrant, LGBT, people of color. One service we offer is mental health support, among other things. Otherwise the community wouldn't have anything.

Angel became more involved in activism after surviving the Pulse shooting; starting his own business and speaking out about hate crimes in the LGBT community:

> After the shooting I decided to start my own clothing line and services as a life coach. The money from my clothing line goes to LGBT organizations. I believe education helps reduce hate crimes because it's just not Pulse; its lack of sex education in our schools, gun control, immigration, and poverty.

Natasha also talked at length about the activist work she has done since the Pulse shooting and connecting with the issue of mental health:

> I was close to the event manager at Pulse, so I came in as a volunteer with #One Pulse, and later an employee. Pulse One has an interim memorial and museum, created to honor the victims of the shooting and for people to come by. You can reflect. We already have 65,000 visitors-about 300 a day. We also have forty-nine endowed scholarship in name of people who were shot, honoring jobs they

wanted to pursue. For example, Amanda Alver wanted to be a nurse, so we have a nursing scholarship in her name. We also have educational programs, which work with companies to be more inclusive towards LGBT. Since the Pulse shooting people are seeking help for mental health. Churches came together, political figures—they all came out. But it gave ammunition to people who didn't like us. You saw the stigma, some victims families found out they were LGBT after they died. So, in people of color communities, as they come together, they have to deal with mental health, which is taboo. You are socialized that you don't talk to people. Young queer Black/Latinx have more resources, more than when I transitioned eight years ago. But there is still the bullying in schools, the difficulty of getting apartments, jobs. Orlando has gender identity protection, but it's not statewide. Being marginalized you take the bull and keep walking. Or you think, "I wasn't there I shouldn't be bothered by it." It uncovered issues they were there before, financial or living situations. People in therapy are beginning to work again. The shooting highlighted gaps in mental health services for LGBT people of color—not everyone had a seat at the table, it was mainly funders.

Raquel also highlighted the way people in Orlando came together during a time of crisis:

The mayor of Orlando did a great job supporting the LGBT community and the mayor of Orange County, while not fan of LGBT community, realized these people could have been their children. We needed donations, lawyers-everyone helped. When trump was elected it felt like Pulse again, but the protest was amazing. I don't think a Pulse massacre would happen at another gay club because of all the support. I see the support in the Hispanic Caucus, where I have worked, the LGBT center. I volunteered with the Red Cross, they don't judge. The One Blood Foundation let gay men donate blood if they haven't had sex in a year. I remember how NYC was after 9/11; I was living upper west side. The day after it was a big deal if someone looked at you and said, "Hi." In Orlando people embraced.

She continues by stating:

#One Pulse is a great example of the intersection of mental health care and activism in the form of educational programs, memorials, and mental health services. It is unfortunate that it took a national tragedy to bring attention to the lack of mental health services within LGBT of color communities, but now with the services being provided, more people are using them, hence easing the stigma of mental health distress in communities of color.

Some queer Black and Latinx people are very intentional about the spaces they work, organize, and live in. For example, New York based poet, activist, and educator; JP Howard discussed reading at venues that would be open and supportive of her intersectional poetry on race, gender, and sexuality:

> I am very intentional about where I read my work and tend to read at queer friendly venues. I know if I go to the Nuyorican Poets Cafe and read queer themed poetry I may not get the love from the crowd as I would at a LGBT friendly event.

Community building is important for many Black and Latinx LGBT people healing from collective experiences of violence. Patrisse Cullors, co-founder of Black Lives Matter discussed the importance of community building at the neighborhood level:

> It's important to build community; it's how we lessen violence against Black people, especially LGBT folks. Whatever policy happens, if there is a leader supporting queer community it's so important; queer youth of color are pushed out of churches, homes, and schools, and on top of that criminalized. Gentrification adds to people feeling unsafe-it feeds people not having a connection with each other. I live in South Central Los Angeles, when I moved there I made it a point to know all my neighbors.

Building community in neighborhoods is important for LGBT Black and Latinx people to create a sense of safety where they live. However, some Black trans women have observed that, albeit three Black women founded Black Lives Matter, two being queer identified, the media focus still seems to be on Black cisgender men being killed by the police (Jacobs 2017; Bordoaro and Willlts 2018).

In the book *Toxic Silence: Race, Black Gender Identity, and Addressing the Violence against Black Transgender Women in Houston*, William T. Houston uses ethnographic methods to interview four Black transgender women on their views on violence within the Black community against them. Many expressed their frustrations with Black Lives Matter, an organization they felt should protect them more. One woman in the study, Mia Ryan, had the following to say regarding Black Lives Matter:

> I respect that a queer woman help start the organization, but let's be honest, how effective has the BLM been to stop violence in the Black community? They only try to protect Black men from white police officers. (Houston 2018: 131)

Lillian mirrored this critique of BLM by underscoring the following:

> I like what BLM is trying to do, but I don't like that they don't fight on behalf of Black trans women. It's obvious that there is a hierarchy in the order of which Black lives really matter.

It is worth mentioning here a discussion at the SF Pride Forum with Alicia Garza, co-founder of Black Lives Matter, on the issue of what Black Lives Matter is doing for Black trans people, to which she responded with the following:

> We're not doing anything for Black trans folks. We want to create a space where Black trans folks can lead.[2]

Hence, Garza is calling for the participation of Black trans people to create and restructure our society to value Black trans lives. I asked Patrisse what she thinks of these observations, especially the conflict within some members of BLM with queer people (i.e., the video that surfaced of Sandra Bland expressing problematic views of LGBT people). How does she bring her full self into movement work often dominated by straight cisgender men? Her response was the following:

> Sometimes I address this issue gracefully; sometimes I am not. I think one has to have an understanding of what's possible, what's needed in a given time. I spend very little time thinking about conflict-I try to build relationships with different people. I have found this to be effective when working with different people in a movement. I have had to fight against erasure in a movement I helped to create.

The marginalization of Black women, especially queer Black women, in social movements resembles the Civil Rights Movement, where Black women's issues were viewed secondary compared to Black men's issues. The current protests of Black trans women[3] demanding justice and recognition is part of this movement to center on Black women's issues.

Through the work of people like Patrisse Cullors and Alicia Garza, the Black Lives Matter movement has become more inclusive of trans rights, which helps to create a political platform for Black trans women experiencing everyday forms of violence both in their communities and on an institutional level. It is obvious that prisons are not the answer to anti-LGBT violence and many queer Black and Latinx people are exploring other options for people who commit hate crimes to be held accountable. This topic will be explored in the next chapter.

CONCLUSION

In this chapter, I examined how hate crimes impact the mental health of queer Black and Latinx people and how this affects their activism. Sylvia

Guerrero experienced mental distress that rendered her unable to work, and receive disability benefits, after the murder of her transgender daughter. Some interviewees, such as Veronica and Nia, avoid social media where they are likely to see a reporting of an anti-LGBT hate crime against a person of color. After Zoraida Reyes' murder, many LGBT Latinx people in Orange County California became more active, while some Latinx trans women distanced themselves from her murder, believing it would not happen to them. In the case of the Orlando Pulse nightclub shooting in Florida, people came together, with many within the LGBT community taking a leading role in volunteering at various organizations, helping people with housing, mental health services, and the building of a memorial in honor of those who were shot.

Yet, inequalities were exposed when exploring how the survivors of the Pulse shootings accessed services. Raquel acknowledged that survivors of the Pulse massacre received housing, but noted that it wasn't in the best of neighborhoods and wondered if white LGBT survivors of a mass shooting would receive the same substandard resources.

However, many struggle to find community. Grant felt his community abandoned him in times of need after surviving a hate crime in Oakland, California, and that the police could not decipher the perpetrators from the victim since Black males were involved. Many survivors of hate crimes like Grant suffer from PTSD and struggle to find safe spaces where their racial, gender, and sexual identities can be affirmed. J. P. Howard navigates this by performing her poetry in queer-friendly spaces, while Patresse Cullors centers on community building among Black people in her Los Angeles neighborhood as a source of strength and resource connection. This chapter focused on the resiliency of individual survivors of violence, the impact of hate crimes on communities, and the resources involved helping survivors access mental health services. However, my findings also point to the shortcomings of the state, whether it is lack of services provided by nonprofits to LGBT populations or slow responses from law enforcement when violence happens.

NOTES

1. Parsley, J. (2019) "Two Pulse Survivors Organize March for Ex-Gays in Orlando." South Florida News. August.
2. Black Lives Matter + the LGBTQI Community: INFORUM + SFPride. https://www.youtube.com/watch?v=6NjVvBejXHI
3. On June 15, 2020, in front of the Brooklyn Arts Museum, a gathering of 15,000 people marched in support of Black Trans Lives.

Chapter 6

Community Justice for LGBT Black and Latinx People

> We have to connect state violence and intimate violence. The cycle of individual harm and violence mirrors state and government level violence, land occupation, history and trauma. There is white violence in the form of mass shootings among white people. This is not particular to Black people; we are just hyper-pathologized. We live in a culture of violence, rape and intergenerational harm.
>
> (Interview with Patrisse Cullors, Co-Founder of Black Lives Matter)

Black and Latinx LGBT communities like their racial communities overall have a fraught relationship with law enforcement. This tension can be seen when violence happens to queer people of color and the police attempts to further victimize them via criminalization. This was the case in 2006 when a group of seven Black lesbians from Newark, New Jersey went to Greenwich Village in New York, and was confronted by a Black cisman who attacked them, including choking one of the girls. One of the girls, Patresse Johnson, stabbed the man with a steak knife attempting to defend her friends. Instead of being portrayed as a heroine, she and her friends were labeled "lesbian killers," and the four women who refused to plead guilty to a reduced sentence served collectively fourteen years in prison.[1]

Stereotypes of LGBT people as sex offenders have long permeated the general public's imagination and resulted in the unfair incarceration of queer people. An example of this is the case of Elizabeth Ramirez, Cassandra Rivera, Kristie Mayhugh, and Anna Vasquez, four Latinx lesbians whom in 1994 were accused of the sexual assault of Ramirez's two nieces. In this case homophobia and satanic witch-hunt ideology contributed to the jury

65

finding these four women guilty of sexual assault and receiving fifteen- to thirty-seven-year sentences (Esquenaz 2016). Hence, queer people of color who experienced hate crimes would hesitate to call the police because of these inequalities within our legal system. In the book *Queer (In) Justice: The Criminalization of LGBT People in the United States*, the authors point out that the queer liberation movement started with fighting police violence, rather that was trans women of color fighting police harassment in the Stonewall riots, or against the criminalization of sex workers, especially trans women of color. While the 2003 *Lawrence vs. Texas* Supreme Court ruling decriminalized gay sex within the private sphere, queer people still are targets of police violence and raids regarding public sexual activity considered to be socially deviant, such as sex work or cruising sites.

Hence, Black and Latinx queer people who have experienced hate crimes may be reluctant to rely on the state for assistance when the state is also responsible for criminalizing them. This is how Lillian felt regarding the role of the police and reporting hate crimes:

> The justice system fails the community, especially the trans community. The police go after innocent Black men; they attack trans women in the form of criminalizing sex workers. If you have a criminal charge, you can't find work, or pay courts back; some have to register as sex offenders. You are placed in the wrong cell, and fear for life. Domestic violence is not taken seriously, that is a hate crime, but not seen as hate crime, but crimes of passion.

Lillian's comment underscores the logic behind the trans and gay panic defense arguments used in courts to minimize hate crimes against queer and trans people, and instead frame them as crimes of passion. In the case of many trans-related hate crimes, one of the most common themes is that of deception where the perpetrator was "tricked."

Angel also doesn't view the police as a reliable source of protection against hate crimes, when he remembers how long it took them to respond to the shootings at the Pulse nightclub:

> The suspect entered the club and started shooting at 2:02 am; at 2:06 am was the last call for alcohol. At 2:07am he started shooting people in the bathrooms. At 2:10 officers entered the club and shot at him, but then shooting stopped and for the next three hours we were trapped with him. He was shooting people in the bathroom. Police took a while to rescue people from the bathroom and did not shoot him until 5:14am. That is too long!

Angel's frustration with the lack of police response mirrors the lack of effective policing in Black and Latinx urban communities. According to a study published from Vanderbilt University individuals with darker skin tones in the Caribbean and Latin America reported a longer police response time (Cohen et al. 2015). Similar feelings of police distrust are of course found in the United States, in the perceptions of both over- and under-policing of Black and Latinx communities. Many Black and Latinx queer people feel victimized and blamed by law enforcement when they report hate crimes. Lupita, a queer gender nonconforming Latinx person had her car vandalized with a swastika someone carved; she is the only overt looking queer woman in a neighborhood of mainly working class Latino males, so she feels she was targeted because of her sexuality and gender identity, which makes it a hate crime:

> I didn't want to file a police report at first because I didn't want a young man of color to go to jail, but friends kept saying I should to document it. So, I went to the police station and spoke to a Latino cop who wasn't really taking me seriously, even after showing him photos of my car. He kept asking me. "Are you sure it was a hate crime, because if it is we will take it more seriously." I told him I thought it was and he said, "Okay, we will send some people out and question some of the neighbors." To this date nothing has happened, but I felt really uncomfortable with the idea that the police would question my neighbors, who I don't trust anyway. I think I know who did this—someone's kids with mental health issues. I wouldn't want this young man to go to jail, so in a way what good was calling the police?

In the case of Lupita reporting the hate crime to the police placed her in potential danger by having police question neighbors who may further harass her, and are distrusting of police. Lupita's hesitancy in calling the police on someone with possible mental health issues supports the activist call to defund the police, and place resources into social workers, who may be better able to assess the situation.

Many Black and Latinx LGBT people view police presence as increasing dangers they face. This was how P. felt when they reported being attacked at a concert in New York and was misgendered by the security guard on duty. Some people are undocumented, or may have a criminal record, which would prevent them from reporting hate crimes to the police, especially since often the perpetrators are in close contact with the survivor (i.e., neighbor, landlord, or partner).

Hence, many queer Black and Latinx people do not trust police to assist them or take seriously reports of hate crimes. This means that they are invested in other methods of holding perpetrators of hate crimes accountable that do not involve the prison industrial complex.

RESTORATIVE JUSTICE MODELS

The history of restorative justice within Canada and the United States dates back to the 1970s as a mediation process between survivors and offenders. Coined by the English it is meant to restore the harmful effects of offender's actions, and involves restoring the relationship between offender and survivor, and performs damage control concerning victim harm (Gavrielides 2012). Restorative justice has its roots in Native American and African communities where dialogue takes place to solve a problem. It has been used in schools to address student misbehavior and involve offenders, survivors of violence, and the community—similar to the criminal justice system's use of restorative justice. The model of justice is based on repairing the relationships of all involved (Payne and Welch 2013). For families, communities, and survivors of hate crimes this form of justice can be healing, even if for some it's a concept not yet tried. For example, when I asked Bamby Salcedo her thoughts on restorative justice, she stated that:

> I have not tried restorative justice, but I am willing to try it. I don't think violence should be met with violence, and that's what you get with our justice system.

For Black and Latinx queer activists who have tried this method, it can be a long process. Patrisse Cullors states that:

> Restorative justice practices can be successful because not everybody feels seen or heard. We have not built a culture yet of understanding; we want blood. But what about long term transformation? I have seen situations where people put in 20 years of work and see the outcome 15 years later.

Cullors' comment underscores the time that must be placed in community healing between families and is not a quick fix like the prison system presents itself to be, which incarcerates people without rehabilitation.

Sylvia Guerrero believes that restorative justice can lead to understanding between families of victims/survivors of hate crimes and perpetrators. For the past fourteen years she visited one of the men in prison who killed her daughter:

> I have visited Jose Merel because he has shown remorse. When the documentary, "Trained in the Ways of Men," about the murder trial came out, his family was in the audience. They didn't identify themselves, but they were there.

Sylvia's choice to visit Merel, who in 2016 was paroled with her support, is based on the fact that he has shown remorse, while the other men involved in her daughter's murder have not. Therefore, she does not visit them, and feels they should remain in prison. Thus, the feeling expressed by some survivors is that perpetrators should remain behind bars if they do not show remorse, and could be a threat to society.

Some participants felt that in addition to perpetrators being sentenced to prisons, there should be classes offered to help rehabilitate them. Natasha felt that there should be consequences to harming someone, which could mean prison, but also there should be an educational process of transformation:

> If you send them to jail, they need to take classes about the history of the people they attacked. The hatred comes from somewhere.

Amber felt that the criminal justice system was corrupted, and that society should invest in people instead of locking them up:

> The criminal justice system is so corrupt on many levels, if we were invested in helping people the system would look different. It depends on the crime they committed, like murder, rape, homophobic hate crimes are all related to assault. But if we taught kids to meditate in school, and not place them in detention, the violence would go down. We would be teaching men to be more compassionate. As long as there is phobia that exist out of prisons we will have hate crimes. Violence against women is not considered a hate crime, but it is. As James Baldwin and Audre Lorde discussed in an interview, if a black boy kills another Black boy, the fact that they were both shoved into this community of violence is not their fault . . . but he is responsible for killing that boy. I also don't believe in the death penalty because when a cop murders someone it s sanctioned by the state.

Charles Brack, the director of the documentary "Dreams Deferred: The Sakia Gunn Film Project," which is about the murder of Sakia Gunn, also questioned the effectiveness of prisons:

> Some people need to be separated from the population—but setting people up for prison is not the right answer. Sakia's mother forgave Richard McCullough in court victim statements. The bottom line is that we have to take responsibility as a community.

Marta Cunningham also questioned the effectiveness of prisons and juvenile detention centers, especially when it concerns children being tried as adults:

> I believe you have to look at a situation holistically. I attended the trials of Brandon McInerney during the King case. People asked me how I could have

sympathy for white supremacist and I told them Brandon came from a violent home. King also came from a challenging home—both are products of families affected by drugs. Where are the resources to help these families? The answer is not to lock up people and sentence kids as adults.

Raquel believed that while some people should be in prison, there needs to be programs for them:

> We have to allow the justice system to do their job, have a case go to trial by a judge, and put them in soldiery confinement. They should not interact with other prisoners. But teach them something. Also, they should have HIV testing 30 days before release. We need to tell them what opportunities are out there—especially women in prison.

Sheila Jackson felt that conversations about trauma need to happen for Black cisgender men who murder Black trans women:

> If we had community members, and therapists we could have some conversations: What were the triggers? Trauma. A lot of Black men have been sexually assaulted, so they project that onto Black trans women. Some Black men sleep with trans women, and slap them in the morning.

In the Netflix documentary *Disclosure*, Laverne Cox discusses the fear and violence toward Black transgender women from some cisgender Black men as a form of projecting their subjugated masculine status in a racist society. These men view Black trans women as the racist embodiment of Black cisgender men being emasculated and project this violence onto the bodies of Black trans women. Education about gender, sexuality, and mental health services were common themes reflected in the literature on hate crimes, rehabilitation, and restorative justice (Perry 2001). In addition to restorative justice techniques and educational resources, some participants felt other forms of societal intervention were necessary in curbing hate crimes.

SHAMING AS A FORM OF PUNISHMENT

Scholars of shame punishment argue that shaming is an alternative to prison for crimes that would receive short prison sentences and replace physical punishment with damage to reputation (Kahan 2005). However, for crimes involving physical assault and/or murder the use of shaming as a form of punishment depends upon if the people attacked are valuable members of society. According to John Braithwaite:

> What matters, according to the theory, is moral clarity in a culture about the evil of killing other people . . . It is why television that communicates the message that the best way to deal with violence is through violence, that those who wrong us can sometimes deserve to die for it, is a problem. Sadly, the ethnographic evidence is that murderers in America often believe they are agents of justice, purifying the world of the evil person they are wasting. (Braithwaite 1989)

Hence, for shaming to be effective the society as a whole would have to value the lives of the people murdered. In a society where the lives of queer Black and Latinx people are not valued, the use of this method is questionable. Lillian agreed that shaming for the murder of Black trans women should not be a tacit, since many Black cisgender men are shamed for dating Black trans women[2]:

> I think [cis] men that kill Black trans women should be shamed within the larger community, instead of being shamed for dating trans women. That would send a message that killing us is unacceptable.

However, some participants argued that shaming reinforces violence against Black and Latinx LGBT people. Sheila felt that shaming as a way to punish mirrors the shame connected to cisgender men who date trans women from Black cisgender women:

> [Cisgender] women should stop shaming men for being who they are—women shame men for being queer. When I was in Atlanta a lady had distain for me, and wanted to get the guy she was with to attack me, and he didn't. She called him a punk and faggot. "You want to fuck her?" [Cisgender] Women have provoked men to attack us. Women befriend us and find out about the men in our lives, and put them on blast. Sometimes you have to keep who you are dating a secret. My mother had a best friend who was trans, they starting working together at Walgreens. She was dating this guy and met some of his family members, when the father learned she was trans his father killed her.

Sheila's comment underscores how the act of shaming is used to justify killing trans women, hence shaming as a form of justice building for the trans community should be questioned. Similarly, the role of cisgender women in instigating violence against trans women is overlooked in many criminal cases.[3] Black trans women are not only threatening to cisgender Black men, but also cisgender heterosexual Black women who view Black trans women as competition.

Sheila also highlights how shame and violence functions to keep Black trans women criminalized within the justice system:

> In Orlando, Florida, where I am from, a lot of trans groups are not published for fear of violence. We moved a trans Black woman to another state because of fear; the police are corrupted. If trans women are stopped on the street, they take off their wigs, if they have falsies they take them out. Police are bad to poor people in San Francisco; they were taking people's tent's away. Survivors of hate crimes in Florida have been attacked going to the supermarket, to Ross, going to the food stamp office. Trans people didn't access food stamps because of harassment; you have a female name but male gender on your ID. Trans women are not allowed to use the restroom. Of course many of us are in the criminal justice system when our access to basic resources is cut off.

The police serve as the largest source of shaming among Black trans women, so when Black and Latinx trans women experience hate crimes, they continue to be violated by the criminal justice system. However, as Sheila's comment illustrates, this societal shaming extends into the welfare office, bathrooms, grocery and clothing stores, keeping trans women from accessing basic services.

COMMUNITY JUSTICE FOR LGBT BLACK AND LATINX COMMUNITIES

According to Adam Crawford and Todd R. Clear, community justice differs than that of restorative justice because the latter is concerned with "the process of outcomes attached to 'cases' of crime . . . It works at the level of a particular criminal cases, seeking to alter how they are handed and how they are resolved" (Crawford and Clear 2003). In contrast, community justice involves the experiences of people living and working in a community. According to Crawford and Clear, "community justice may be seen as having a more radical reform orientation than restorative justice. It holds its advocates accountable not only for the handling of cases but for the nature of collective experience" (ibid.).

For Black and Latinx LGBT people, the collective matters, along with the environment many of them live and work in, which extends beyond individual, hate crime cases. For many queer and trans Black and Latinx people violence starts at the structural levels (i.e., employment, education, housing, and health care). Sheila discusses the challenges of Black trans women, especially formerly incarcerated, in San Francisco when receiving gender affirmation surgery at Kaiser Permanente, or finding housing:

> There are many challenges for trans women who have been in prison—one is having access to employment, knowing where to go, so you don't go back into the street. Many trans girls come in and out of jail for selling drugs. In our organization we get in touch with community members who are abolitionist; we house people in hotels, the county has money to house people, but no one contacted us. I have to fire some women because they don't have housing, and are not showing up to work.

Sheila's comments illustrates that justice is not just about individual rights, and punishment for a crime, but the transformation of structures, and the un-othering of Black and Latinx LGBT within them.

OTHERING AS A FORM OF VIOLENCE AND THE REFRAMING OF COMMUNITY

In the article, "Gender and Genocide in Rwanda: Women as Agents and Objects of Genocide," Sharlach (1999) challenges the identity of women as being naturally pacific and that the only identity they are operating within is one of their gender. In examining the Rwandan genocide Sharlach argues that:

> The participation of so many Hutu women in the 1994 killings in Rwanda lends little support, however, to the essentialist stance that women are innately pacific. (pp. 396–397)

This challenge of gender loyalty is important because it gives context to identities beside gender that are in effect when women commit violence against other women. In this case ethnicity/tribal affiliation was more important than gender, with the media further underscoring differences between Hutu and Rwandan women. The connection of hate crimes against Black/Latinx trans women and genocide is also not far-fetched given the high numbers of murders within this group (Kidd and Witten 2008). When it comes to violence against Black trans women from Black cisgender people, this analysis helps to explain that trans Black women are othered by some cisgender Black women, to underscore their womanhood; cisgender Black men, both other and murder Black trans women, to protect their manhood. In order for violence against Black and Latinx LGBT people to stop, especially for Black and Latinx trans women, they would have to be integrated within their communities, and the larger society.

Since the murders of James Byrd Jr., Matthew Shepard, and Gwen Araujo, there have been federal and local state efforts to include gender identity in hate crime law and enhance punishment (i.e., longer sentencing). However, this has not stopped hate crimes from happening nor has it decreased the numbers; in fact, hate crimes have increased under President Trump, especially with respect to transgender women of color. There are many reasons for the continuation of hate crimes (racism, sexism, transphobia, homophobia, xenophobia), but the one I will focus on is the marginalization of queer Black and Latinx people within community and societal institutions, especially educational systems, health care facilities, and churches.

TRANSFORMING EDUCATIONAL INSTITUTIONS FOR BLACK AND LATINX STUDENTS

According to the article, "Hate Crimes on Campuses Is Rising, New FBI Data Shows," by Dan Bauman, 280 hate crimes were reported on college campuses in 2017, an increase from 257 in 2016 (Bauman 2018). Yet, hate crime numbers are underreported because of fear and lack of information on how to file complaints (Potok 2000). This was what happened to Veronica, leading her to become an activist even after facing death threats. Colleges and universities market themselves on liberal ideas and embracing diversity; this is evident on campus brochures and other promotional materials illustrating students of diverse backgrounds learning in a safe environment. However, for many queer Black and Latinx students the classroom and overall college environment does not feel safe. This is supported by survey results conducted by the Association of American Universities published in the 2015 *Atlantic* article, "LGBT Students and Sexual Assault," by Adrienne Green and Alia Wong:

> While sexual violence is the most overt of violence for queer students on college campuses, many LGBT Black and Latinx people are marginalized in other ways in university settings, increasing their chances of being targets for hate crimes. (Green and Wong 2015)

The lack of LGBT content in classes outside of gender studies reinforces that LGBT issues are not important in the classroom, and when discussing Black and Latinx LGBT issues, race needs to be reflected in college curriculum. Furthermore, colleges and universities need to have LGBT and race antidiscrimination policies as part of their strategic plan.

In the article "Improving the Climate for LGBTQ Students at an Historically Black University," by Marilyn W. Lewis and Kirsten S. Ericksen, the issue of avoidance of LGBT issues by faculty and staff marginalized Black LGBT students, and gives the impression that they are not welcomed on the campus (Lewis and Ericksen 2016).

The need for faculty and staff to be trained in LGBT and racial diversity issues is critical in and outside of the classroom. As I stated in an NBC article about college climate for LGBT students, the curriculum of the classroom also determines if LGBT students are welcomed on a campus.[4] If the curriculum is not LGBT inclusive within various fields, this further marginalizes LGBT students, especially Black and Latinx students who often experience racial isolation in classrooms.

For trans Black and Latinx college students access to higher education is a challenge; as illustrated from Lillian's interview, many Black and Latinx trans people, especially women, do not have access to higher education. Filling out financial aid forms, college applications where potential students may not have their gender identity match with state IDs, immigration status, and lack of family support all create structural barriers to trans Black and Latinx people achieving higher education. For queer Black and Latinx students that are in the university, fear of violence and harassment results in many leaving colleges and universities.

However, the challenges that plague Black and Latinx students begin before college starting in the K-12 school systems. The fight to have both Ethnic Studies and LGBT studies in public schools is an ongoing debate involving parents, local and state politicians, and students. In Arizona, controversy over the inclusion of a Mexican American program in the Tucson Unified School District underscores this debate with two former state members of the school superintendents feeling that such a program was divisive, and others feeling the program will close the achievement gap of Latino/a students (Anderson 2016). Similarly, LGBT inclusion in public school has been resisted with parents fighting for religious freedom, teachers not feeling comfortable with the topic, and school boards refusing to teach LGBT-related material. Yet, things are slowly changing with states such as California including LGBT friendly textbooks within elementary schools (Allen 2017). This change would have affected the experience of Latisha King in Oxnard, California, who attended E.O. Green Middle School, where teachers, staff, and students marginalized and bullied King, and administrators still refuse to discuss the case.[5]

In addition to racial and queer inclusive classes in K-12 school systems, trans students of color need financial assistance, forms that are inclusive of their gender identity, housing, employment, gender neutral bathrooms, student centers, and health resources. The creation of these resources on K-12 and college campuses will reduce feelings of marginalization and hopefully hate crimes against trans students.

HEALTH CARE FOR ALL: MAKING MEDICAL
INDUSTRIES LGBT AND RACIALLY INCLUSIVE

Many LGBT Black and Latinx people face challenges to accessing health care, from lack of health insurance, racism of medical professionals, dearth of training serving Black/Latinx LGBT communities, and institutionalized homo/transphobia during patient intakes (Follins and Lassiter 2017). In my interviews with participants, many noted health care challenges, whether it was barriers to Black/Latinx trans women receiving hormones, like Sheila pointed out, or not being able to afford gender affirmation surgery, or just not having access to health care period because of unemployment, which both Lillian and P. discussed in their interviews. Racial stereotyping of Black and Latinx people also impedes access to health care and feeling safe with medical staff.

Veronica recently went to the hospital with chest pain, and a male Asian doctor continuously asked her if she was depressed. Then he started discussing HIV medication with her, stating that it can be reversed, and asking her how many sex partners she had and if she did drugs:

> I kept saying I have chest pains; I have lupus. I have one same sex partner, who is a woman. He then asked me if I were on drugs because HIV could be transmitted that way as well. I was like, "What?? I have chest pains. What does this have to do with anything?" I know I could have filed a complaint, but I was just trying to survive.

Experiences of not being listened to and racially stereotyped are common for Black women to have within medical establishments. The recent examples of Serena Williams almost dying in childbirth confirms the fears many people of color have about going to doctors, especially LGBT Black and Latinx communities. Trans and gender nonconforming people often hide their gender identity to receive medical care (Poteat and Follins 2016).

Medical establishments can be more racially and queer inclusive by viewing people as individuals even though they come from a certain demographic, and listening to their health concerns. For example, not all health issues are related to someone being trans/gender nonconforming, and not all cisgender women are at risk for HPV. Heteronormative assumptions can make someone feel unconformable, resulting in them not returning to receive medical care. This can be particularly concerning at Christian hospitals, where these messages are more pronounced.

For instance, I remember going for my annual checkup at a Christian identified hospital, and at the bottom of the summary of my visit there were a list of things related to taking care of one's health. One line stated that women should always wear condoms when sexually active, and be married when thinking of starting a family. I went back to the doctor's office and informed the doctor, who was an Asian cisgender woman, that this pamphlet isn't appropriate for everyone, especially queer women. She apologized stating that this was a standard form given to everyone that comes in. Hopefully, this office will rethink the messages in their literature and how this can make people who are queer and/or color uneasy.

Health care clinics and offices can have queer and racially diverse material on the office walls and desk of staff members. In addition to materials, a diverse staff is necessary to understand how to treat clients and make them feel seen. Language is also important, terms such as "homosexual," and "transsexual" are outdated and can make people feel not welcomed. Furthermore, health care professionals need to be trained on how to serve people of color, especially Black and Latina cisgender women. Associating disease and drug use with women of color, especially trans women of color is deeply problematic, especially if women have had a history of drug use— their identity gets reduced to that. Health care workers need to be diverse and trained to deal with both queer and people of color populations, not appearing to be unconformable with the social, medical, and sexual histories of LGBT clients of color (Martos et al. 2018).

Mental health professionals also need to be trained to serve LGBT Black and Latinx populations, this is especially important for queer youth of color. Many LGBT youth of color are in conflict with their families about their identities, but economically depended upon them. Research shows that transgender youth experience more school harassment, homelessness, anxiety, depression, and suicidality (McCann and Sharek 2016). Therapists must be informed of how the intersection of various identities affects the mental health of LGBT Black and Latinx populations—especially the role of religion when negotiating identities of race, sexuality, class, and gender identity.

RELIGIOUS INSTITUTIONS AND COMMUNITY ACCEPTANCE

The most influential institution for many LGBT Black and Latinx people is the church; compared to other racial groups, 87 percent of Black people identify as religious (Taylor et al. 2014). For Black people the church has played an important role in fostering a sense of community, resources, and social justice; since slavery the Black Church has provided Black communities with social support to deal with racism, assist in mental health, and help with community activism. For Latinx people religion also plays a strong role in their lives according to the Pew Hispanic survey, 83 percent claiming a religious affiliation, usually identifying as Catholic. However, in spite of the historic community building of the church, it remains a problematic institution for many queer Black and Latinx people. This was evident during the Pulse massacre shooting with some church leaders implying that the Pulse victims were living in sin and got what they deserved. While this was not a dominant view, and many in the religious community in Orlando and nationally condemned the violence, the fact that many religious communities view the LGBT community as sinful cannot be understated.

For instance, days after the shooting, Pastor Roger Jimenez of Verity Baptist Church in Sacramento posted a YouTube video stating that Christians should not morn the "death of 50 sodomites . . . the tragedy is that more of them didn't die . . . I think that's great" (Bever 2016). Another pastor in Fort Worth, Donnie Romero of Stedfast Baptist Church prayed that the victims would die in intensive care (Stewart 2018). These statements underscore the antigay teachings of the religious right, and the normalization of hatred of queer people via using conservative religious readings to justify that the LGBT community should not exist. Religious marginalization of queer people of color is global with examples in Uganda, South Africa, Latin America, and the Caribbean; this marginalization is the result of centuries of colonization from missionaries. Unfortunately, in this construction of religious doctrine, queer Black and Latinx people become the scapegoat for problems in the community and a barometer for moral behavior. This scapegoating encourages people from within religious communities to abuse power and create hierarchies of humanity, which function to exclude and create boundaries of group membership.

However, this analysis is not meant to imply that Black and Latinx communities are more homo/transphobic than the larger white communities. In fact, when one examines the data the opposite is true. According to data from the Public Religion Research Institute, "Fewer than half of white evangelical Protestants (43 percent) and Mormons (49 percent) believe gays and lesbians experience discrimination. Whereas, Black Americans (three-quarters) are more likely to perceive discrimination against LGBT people, and two-thirds of Latinx people perceive discrimination against LGBT people" (Jones et al. 2017). A recent example of white liberals using the narrative of Black homophobia as obstructing white political gain is the debate regarding Black support for democratic Presidential Candidate Pete Buttigieg who is gay, and his lack of Black supporters, who are framed as not supporting him because they are homophobic, instead of political concerns they may have about his stance on issues affecting Black people (Capehart 2019).

My highlighting of the religious conservatism that exists among some Black and Latinx communities is to emphasize the role of capitalism and heterosexism in marginalizing Black and Latinx LGBT members within communities of color. Most Black and Latinx LGBT people live among their larger ethnic communities, and not in the white communities, which hold the political power to institutionalize hetero-supremacy, and violence against Black and Latinx LGBT people in the form of laws, restriction of health care services, and housing.

According to Cathy Cohen and Tamara Jones in the essay, "Fighting Homophobia verses Challenging Heterosexism: The Failure to Transform Revisited," they argue that the function of heterosexism in Black communities is based on capitalism, with a dominant group keeping most of the cultural resources by constructing queer people as an "other" within Black institutions (Cohen and Jones 1999). This analysis is important to understanding heterosexism as being rooted in capitalism, white supremacy, and patriarchy. When examining community attitudes around queerness, and antigay rhetoric in some Black and Latinx religious settings, the connection to resources and racism is important to linking ideology and the obtaining of material resources for working class Black and Latinx communities (Hutchinson 2011).

It is not a coincidence that in poor/working class Black and Latinx communities, churches are the main institution allowed to flourish in under-resourced neighborhoods. This is true in Black urban communities that lack Black owned businesses; there are several churches in lieu of other institutions to serve the community. Given the social and economic reality that makes churches necessary in communities of color, this is a powerful institution to transform hate crimes against Black and Latinx communities. Similar work has been done involving churches when it comes to the issue of HIV/AIDS in Black communities (Quinn et al. 2016). Also, churches in Black and Latinx communities that convey messages of LGBT acceptance and social justice can shift how queer Blacks and Latinx lives are valued within and outside of their environment (Winder 2015).

Fortunately, more churches in Black and Latinx communities are LGBT friendly, such as First Corinthian Baptist Church in Harlem, the Black Church movement, Many Voices: A Black Church Movement for Gay and Transgender Justice,[6] East Bay Church of Religious Science in Oakland, California, and the United Fellowship of Metropolitan Community Churches. Similar to the acceptance of LGBT students at Historically Black Colleges and Universities (HBCUs), religious institutions are key in fostering a sense of racial and ethnic belonging for LGBT Black and Latinx communities. The acceptance isn't always immediate, but this inclusion sends an important message that queer people are part of the larger community, and that their lives matter, continuing a trajectory of social justice and the fight for equality.

CONCLUSION

In this chapter, I explored the connections between everyday violence, the criminal justice system, restorative justice models, and transforming community institutions in Black and Latinx neighborhoods. Many LGBT Black and Latinx survivors of physical violence do not feel safe reporting to the police, fearing further abuse and possibly being a target for violence in their neighborhoods, if someone in the neighborhood attacked them. Some feel uncomfortable using the state to confront hate crimes, when much of the violence queer Black and Latinx people experienced comes from the state (police shootings and sexual assault, educational marginalization, unemployment, homelessness). Punitive hate crime laws also have not decreased violence, with people coming out of prison sometimes worse than they were before, and without rehabilitation education. Some felt that restorative justice was effective in reducing hate crimes and trying to get perpetrators to see the harms they have caused to individuals and communities.

I underscored the importance of challenging white, cisgender, and hetero-supremacy within educational institutions, health care, and religious spaces. The origins of everyday violence against Black and Latinx LGBT people can be found in these three institutions where LGBT Black and Latinx people are marginalized within and outside of their racial/ethnic communities. In health care institutions many providers are not trained on the needs of the LGBT community and/or hold racist stereotypes of people of color, which prevent them from providing them with the best service. Many Black and Latinx trans women are mistreated and not given the care they seek, whether it's being denied surgeries, or being misgendered. Black cisgender and trans women are often viewed as hypersexualized with their health needs revolving around the belief that they are on drugs, have multiple sex partners, or do not know their own bodies. In other words, doctors do not listen to them.

In educational settings, teachers are either uncomfortable or discouraged from teaching Ethnic Studies and/or LGBT content in their classes, even while LGBT Black and Latinx children are bullied at school. Sometimes, bullying leads to physical violence or death for LGBT Black and Latinx children, such as Latisha King who was shot in front of students and a teacher in a computer class at E.O. Green Middle School in Oxnard, California, or the suicide of transgender teen Blake Brockington, who was a student at

University of North Carolina at Charlotte. While colleges and universities are supportive of Black, Latinx, and LGBT centers and interdisciplinary fields, such as Ethnic Studies/Gender Studies, and Queer Studies, the presence of these groups is still marginalized within the classroom and the larger college campus. In California, there is a current proposal to include Ethnic Studies and LGBT courses within the K-12 system, and the Cal State system voted to have Ethnic Studies courses be required for graduation.[7] In addition, HBCUs are including queer content and admitting transgender students into gender specific colleges (i.e., all women's or all men's colleges). These are all steps in the right direction toward institutionalizing Black and Latinx curricular within the K-12th system and higher education in the United States.

Lastly, religious institutions are the main institution that holds the most challenges and promises for LGBT Black and Latinx communities. Unfortunately, Christian Right messages framing queer people as sinful and an abomination are found in many churches across the United States. Since President's Trump's election the Christian Right and the government have attacked LGBT Black and Latinx communities from transgender bathroom laws in North Carolina, to anti-immigration policies, threats to abortion rights, and racialized shootings, such as the recent shootings of mainly Latino immigrants in El Paso, Texas and the shooting of mostly Black people in Dayton, Ohio.

Religious institutions in Black and Latinx communities are important in how LGBT people are framed as part of the community; when pastors and priest make disparaging remarks toward queer people the message is that LGBT Black and Latinx people are not part of the larger community, or that they are sinful and/or loved in spite of their sin but not fully accepted. This is dangerous because if a hate crime happens there can be ambivalence in how the larger community responds or a feeling that queer Black and Latinx individuals bring hate crimes and violence onto themselves by acting deviant. Fortunately, some religious institutions are fostering messages of love and acceptance, with LGBT individuals heading some of these churches. Yet, many religious institutions prove to be a major obstacle toward community acceptance of LGBT Black and Latinx people—but hold the greatest hope for community recognition.

NOTES

1. Dorosh-Walther, B. (2014). *Out in the Night*. Fire This Time The Film.
2. On August 19, 2019, Maurice Willoughby in Philadelphia committed suicide after being bullied on social media for dating a Black trans woman.

3. In the murder of Gwen Araujo, the girlfriend of one of the defendant's brothers encouraged and conducted forced gender inspection of Gwen's body, leading to her claiming that Gwen was a man, which led to her attack by four men.

4. Slater Tate, A. Campus Pride: How Colleges Are Welcoming LGBT Students— NBC News, April 23, 2016.

5. Doing research for this book, I tried to speak to the principal of the school, but had no success getting hold of any administrator.

6. https://www.manyvoices.org

7. Symon, E. (2020). "Mandatory Ethnic Studies Course for CSU Graduation Bill Passed by Senate." *California Globe*. June 19.

Conclusion

Everyday violence against Black and Latinx LGBT people is unfortunately a reality, even given the various laws geared to protect them from discrimination, in the states that honor them. But we do not have laws that protect people from physical violence. We also don't have laws that guarantee gainful employment, living wages, health care, safe educational environments, and for some religious validation in their places of worship. During the completion of this book, the Netflix docu-series, "The Trials of Gabriel Fernandez" aired. In this six-part docu-series we are introduced to Gabriel Fernandez, a Latinx boy from Palmdale, California whose parents tortured and murdered him in 2013. The documentary follows Gabriel's abuse at the hands of his mother and her boyfriend, who beat him over an eight-month period resulting in his death. It is suspected that part of the reason he was abused and murdered was because he was perceived to be gay—even though this case was not pursued as a hate crime. It is easy to focus on the horror of the abuse Gabriel's caretakers inflicted upon him, but the system is equally to blame for his death.

Throughout the documentary, we see systemic failure on the part of teachers, social workers, police officers, sheriff departments, and the Los Angeles Department of Child and Family Services. Police reports were not filed during family visits, teachers were told it wasn't their job to investigate child abuse, social workers would not take Gabriel for medical visits to confirm abuse, and the sheriff department withheld information from the District Attorney assigned to the case. In many ways, it is the systemic failure that is most harmful for children such as Gabriel because these systems could have saved him from the individual abused suffered in his family.

This documentary represents the premise of this book—highlighting the individual and systemic violence against LGBT Black and Latinx people within and outside of their ethnic communities. It is easy to blame individual family, community members, and strangers for the physical violence many Black and Latinx LGBT endure, but the systems that LGBT Black and Latinx people live in are equally, if not more, responsible not just for physical forms of violence, but structural everyday violence in the forms of lack of health care, homelessness, unemployment, and lack of access to education. Similarly, while this book examines everyday violence within Black and Latinx communities, the root of this violence does not lie with those communities, but with larger white power structures, which control economic resources in Black and Latinx communities.

When Sakia Gunn was murdered in 2003 she and her friends were at a bus stop less than 100 feet from an empty "24-hour" police kiosk. They were teens waiting for a bus at 3 a.m. coming from Greenwich Village. The spatial disinvestment in social services in Newark created a situation for Gunn to be harassed and murdered. Why did the bus not come? Why was the police kiosk empty in spite of it labeled "24-hours?" This disinvestment speaks to the role of police violating the rights of Black and Latino/a/x communities, as the protests against George Floyd's murder by police in Minneapolis illustrate, along with the Supreme Court's decision to not hear cases challenging police use of qualified immunity, which protects them from lawsuits. Instead, activists have called for defunding the police and placing resources in communities, such as the one Sakia Gunn lived in, toward social programs.

After her murder Newark activists, such as Janyce Jackson, senior pastor of Liberation in Truth Unity Fellowship Church, helped to mobilize the community and create an LGBT space in Newark, New Jersey (Zenzele 2013).

When twenty-eight-year-old Zoraida Reyes was murdered in 2014, her body dumped outside of a fast food restaurant in Anaheim, California, she was unemployed, uninsured, and had to leave UC Santa Barbara because she couldn't afford the tuition. She had reportedly applied for several service sector jobs, but never received a callback because she was an immigrant transgender woman. The structural marginalization of trans women of color like Reyes places them in situations within marginalized economies, such as sex work, which can be dangerous. Additionally, the police did not investigate her murder even though they found it suspicious (Flores 2014).

Gwen Araujo was pushed out of her high school because of bullying and transphobia. She struggled with employment and her religious community also ostracized her—leaving her in precarious situation for resources.

The deaths of the above Black and Latinx individuals share common characteristics—poverty, racism, and transphobia. Black and Latinx people at large tend to live in areas with less wealth, government investment, and more police brutality. They are disproportionately represented within the criminal justice system, pushed out of educational opportunities, and viewed as a social problem instead of a social asset.

In order for violence to cease among LGBT Black and Latinx people, their communities would need more structural support. A reframing of health care systems as part of state violence against Black and Latinx LGBT people is useful; this would expand our definition of what is meant by state violence. For example, there is attention to Black men being killed by police, but not on the numbers of Black queer men still dying of AIDS (Farrow 2016). Black men with HIV are also criminalized instead of getting medical treatment (Greene 2019). Educational institutions need to normalize people of color and LGBT people in the classroom, and real estate markets must stop pushing poor and working class Black and Latinx people out of their homes and into home-lessness where they are at increased risk for physical and psychological harm. Capital should be available for Black and Latinx business entrepreneurs who wish to open up queer venues. The fact that Pulse happened on "Latin Night" speaks to the marginalization of queer people of color in otherwise white queer spaces, where they are relegated to a theme night (i.e., hip-hop, Latin).

In addition, there needs to be a cultural shift in how LGBT Black and Latinx people, especially trans women, are viewed (Garza 2019). Bad Bunny, Janelle Monae, Gabrielle Union, and Dwayne Wade are celebrities who model LGBT acceptance in LGBT Black and Latinx communities. Bad Bunny is a Puerto Rican rapper known for his gender bending performances and support of LGBT people. On *The Tonight Show* with Jimmy Fallon, Bad Bunny brought attention to the murder of Alexa Negrón Luciano, a homeless transgender woman who was murdered in San Juan, Puerto Rico after being accused of spying on women customers in a McDonald's bathroom. Bad Bunny performed wearing a black skirt and a white T-shirt with the words, "They Killed Alexa, Not a Man in a Skirt" in Spanish.

Earlier this year actress Gabrielle Union and former basketball player Dwyane Wade introduced the world to their transgender daughter, Zaya Wade. They have always been supportive of their child's LGBT identity and went to Miami Pride with them as a show of commitment to their child and LGBT issues at large. These celebrity examples of LGBT support in Black and Latinx communities is important to changing the cultural climate that devalues the lives of LGBT Black and Latinx people. Unfortunately, because of racism within white mainstream media, which shows Black people only as homophobic,[1] we see many examples of Black or Latinx celebrities making fun of queer people or condemning them (i.e., Dave Chappelle, Kevin Hart), and not enough examples of those Black and Latinx celebrities across sexuality supporting queer people.

Of course this alone will not stop violence against queer people of color, but these are steps in the right direction since celebrity culture is powerful in shaping people's worldviews. Black and Latino/a activists need to place equal value on sexism and homo/transphobia as they do on racism. A recent example of the consequences of what happens when intersectionality is not centered on race-based movements is the murder of Oluwatoyin Salau. Salau was a nineteen-year-old Black Lives Matter activist, who was homeless and tweeted about being sexually assaulted by a Black man who offered her a ride. Her body was found along with seventy-five-year-old Victoria Sims. Aaron Glee, Jr. was taken into custody for double homicide (Del Rio and McDonnell 2020). Black women's bodies cannot continue to be sacrificed for racial justice.

My goal for this book is twofold: One goal is to foster initiate conversations within Black and Latinx communities regarding LGBT issues and how community support is critical for the well-being of not only LGBT Black and Latinx people, but their larger ethnic communities also. Our families, community centers, and churches can be a place of healing, resource sharing, and progressive leadership for LGBT people. The everyday violence against LGBT Black and Latinx people also affects heterosexual people. Religious fascism, the buttressing of ideas that queerness is associated with sin and deviance, is connected to sexual conservatism. For example, abortion, sexual violence, and sex education are issues the church and larger communities can take on under the frame of LGBT issues. LGBT Black and Latinx people at large face various forms of violence—from the everyday to the physical. Some examples are police shootings, domestic violence, gun violence, absence of LGBT Black and Latinx people within educational curriculum, and overall poverty.

As I stated earlier my focus on hetero-supremacy and/or transphobia within Black and Latinx communities is not to demonize people of color, or ignore the hetero-supremacy of white people and institutions, but to help reframe struggles for racial justice in Black and Latinx communities, to center issues of gender and sexuality. Studies show that most anti-LGBT violence is intra-racial (Stotzer 2013), hence it would make sense that focusing on violence against LGBT Black and Latinx people exposes how they are marginalized within their home communities.

The second goal for this book is to interrogate medical institutions, schools, and employment agencies regarding the needs of LGBT Black and Latinx people. Everyday violence is institutional marginalization, which places queer Blacks and Latinx people lives in peril. The shooting of Latisha King at E.O. Green Junior High School in Oxnard, California illustrates the lack of LGBT issues within school policies leading to violence. Prior to Latisha's murder teachers discouraged them from wearing make-up, citing violations to the dress code. The policing of queer youth supports a school to prison pipeline, which creates economically vulnerable situations for LGBT black and Latinx youth (Snapp et al. 2015). After King's murder the school has not done community outreach to bring more awareness about anti-LGBT violence and the principal chose not to discuss the issue.

Employment is a major issue for many LGBT Black and Latinx people, especially transgender people. The recent Supreme Court decision stating that LGBT are protected from workplace discrimination is a giant step in the direction of eradicating barriers for Black and Latinx LGBT people to find employment. We also need to extend antidiscrimination policies to housing, which is a challenge for many poor/working class LGBT Black and Latinx people, especially youth.

The underemployment of LGBT Black and Latinx people places them in economically precarious situations, such as prostitution, where they are subject to police arrest and street violence and/or abusive relationships. Underemployment makes it hard for LGBT people to provide for themselves, and their families, thus some rely on the state for support (welfare), where they can be subject to more state control. Heterosexual Black and Latino/a people have less wealth than their white counterparts, and queer Black and Latinx people have even less because of racism, transphobia, and hetero-supremacy in the workplace. The lack of jobs with benefits affects the kinds of health queer Black and Latinx people receive, contributing to untreated physical and mental health challenges. Programs such as TransCanWork, Inc., which is a nonprofit based in Los Angeles, help provide transgender people with jobs and offer trans inclusive trainings to employers.

Lastly, health care providers need LGBT and racial sensitivity training when serving LGBT Black and Latinx LGBT people. Research on Black LGBT health issues overwhelming focuses on AIDS/HIV without identifying specific barriers to queer Black men accessing treatment or overall structural issues that places them at risk. Yet, Black and Latinx LGBT issues are more than AIDS/HIV or sexually transmitted diseases. LGBT Black and Latinx people also deal with hypertension, diabetes, cancers, and other health issues that the general public deals with. In addition, some trans people may deal with the effects of hormones, gender affirmation surgeries, cervical and prostate cancer. COVID-19 is a global epidemic disproportionately affecting Black and Latinx LGBT people. They are concentrated in jobs where they either don't have the privilege to work remotely from home, thus being exposed to the virus, or they have been furloughed, adding to the wealth gap.

For many LGBT Black and Latinx people, in addition to the economic consequences of COVID-19, is the structural violence of the health care system. In the beginning of the crisis gay and bisexual men could not donate blood, now this ban has been eased, allowing for queer men to donate blood as long as they have not had sex in three months. Similarly, religious hospitals, such as Mount Sinai Hospital, have a "Statement of Faith," upholding policies against LGBT identities (Metro Weekly 2020). An organization operating out of the hospital, Samaritan's Purse, set up sixty-eight-bed tent hospitals in Central Park to treat COVID-19 positive patients. Yet, LGBT groups remain concerned that the hospital will uphold antidiscrimination policies regarding LGBT people. Furthermore, Black and Latinx LGBT people represent those with pre-health conditions, which makes COVID-19 a serious illness, if not fatal.

Regarding mental health, LGBT Black and Latinx people experience anxiety, depression, and substance abuse from institutional marginalization and violence. Domestic and sexual violence are also concerns for LGBT Black and Latinx people that require culturally competent therapists. The medical field needs to challenge anti-LGBT bias concerning Black and Latinx people. For example, many trans/gender nonconforming people must assume the diagnosis of gender dysphoria to be approved for gender affirmation surgeries. This requirement reinforces beliefs that trans people are deviant—both medically and socially. Furthermore, intake forms and other medical documents need to reflect the identities of LGBT Black and Latinx people, which is why LGBT clinics and providers within Black and Latinx communities are important for overall mental and physical well-being of LGBT Black and Latinx people.

These are the steps our society and communities can take to eradicate the everyday violence experienced by LGBT Black and Latinx people. What is at stake in this project are health care, educational systems, child welfare, families, and working environments providing an equal distribution of resources centering queer Black and Latinx people. Black and Latinx race-based social movements will become stronger once they center the needs of LGBT Black and Latinx people, and white LGBT movements can be more effective in their fight against homo/transphobia by adopting a racial analysis. Thus, the most marginalized within both Black/Latinx communities and LGBT populations will benefit—which is a win for all.

NOTE

1. A recent example of the media portrayal of Black people as homophobic is the Netflix reality series, *Love is Blind*, which follows couples as they speed date. One couple consists of a Black bisexual man who comes out to his Black fiancée, who rejects him after learning his sexuality.

References

Allen, S. 2017. "California Leads the Way Teaching LGBT History to Schoolchildren." *The Daily Beast.* November 14, 2017.

Alokozai, J. 2016. "In Memory of Zoraida Reyes." *Medium.* June 10, 2016.

Alvarez, C., & Fedock, G. 2018. "Addressing Intimate Partner Violence with Latina Women: A Call for Research." *Trauma, Violence, and Abuse, 19*(4), 488–493.

Anderson, M. 2016. "The Ongoing Battle Over Ethnic Studies." *The Atlantic.* March 7, 2016.

Bauman. D. 2018. "Hate Crimes on Campuses Is Rising, New FBI Data Shows," *Chronicle of Higher Education.* November 14, 2018.

Bell, J. G., & Perry, B. 2015. "Outside Looking In: The Community Impacts of Anti-Lesbian, Gay, and Bisexual Hate Crime." *Journal of Homosexuality, 62*(1), 98–120.

Berman, Mark, & Horwitz, Sari. 2015. "George Zimmerman Won't Face Civil Rights Charges in Trayvon Martin's Death." *Washington Post.* February 24, 2015.

Bever, Lindsey. 2016. "Pastor Refuses to Mourn Orlando Victims: 'The Tragedy Is That More of Them Didn't Die'." *The Washington Post.* June 15, 2016.

Boster, M. 2014. "Transgender Woman's Mother, 'Other Family' Mourn her Death. *Los Angeles Times.* June 24, 2014.

Brack, C. 2008. *Dreams Deferred: Sakia Gunn Film Project.* Third World Newsreel.

Braithwaite, J. 1989. *Crime, Shame and Reintegration.* Cambridge University Press.

Branson-Potts. H. 2019. "Ed Buck was Known for his Abrasive Behavior. But Politicians still took his Money." *The Los Angeles Times.* October 17, 2019.

Brekke, K. 2014. "CeCe McDonald Shares Her Struggles of Being a Trans Woman in a Male Prison Facility." Queer Voices. *HuffPost.* May 21, 2014.

Bridges, K. 2011. *Reproducing Race: An Ethnography of Pregnancy as a Site of Racialization.* California: University of California Press.

Browne-Marshall, Gloria J. 2013. *Race, Law and American Society.* New York: Routledge.

Capehart, J. 2019. "The Ugly Lie about Black Voters and Pete Buttigieg" *The Washington Post* Opinion. November 8, 2019.

Cohen, C. J., & Jones, T. 1999. "Fighting homophobia versus challenging heterosexism: The failure to transform" revisited. In *Dangerous Liaisons: Blacks, Gays, and the Struggle for Equality*, pp. 80–101. New York: The New Press.

Cohen, M., Zechmeister, E., & Seligson, M. 2015. *"American's Barometer: Topical Brief: Those with Darker Skin Report Slower Police Response."* Tennessee: Vanderbilt University.

Cowan, Gloria, Resendez, Miriam, Marshall, Elizabeth, & Quist, Ryan. 2002. "Hate Speech and Constitutional Protection: Priming Values of Equality and Freedom." *Journal of Social Issues, 58*(2): 247–263.

Crawford, A., & Clear, T. R. 2003. "Community Justice: Transforming Communities Through Restorative Justice." *Restorative justice: Critical issues*, *3*, 215.

Cruz, Nicole Santa. 2014. "The Homicide Report." *LA Weekly*. October 3, 2014.

Cullen, T. 2018. "Omar Mateen Originally Wanted to Attack Disney Hot Springs with Rifle Hidden in Stroller Before Shooting Up Pulse." *New York Daily News*. March 28, 2018.

Cunningham, M. (2013). *Valentine Road*. HBO.

Dane, Perry. 1943. "West Virginia State Board of Education V. Barnette, 319 US 624 (1943)."

Davis, A. Y. 1982. *Women, Race, & Class*. New York: Vintage.

Del Rio, N. & Gulia McDonnell. 2020. "Oluwatoyin Salauwas, Missing Black Lives Matter Activist, Is Found Dead." *The New York Times*. June 15, 2020.

Dernikos, B. P. 2016. "Queering"# BlackLivesMatter: Unpredictable Intimacies and Political Affects. *SQS–Suomen Queer-tutkimuksen Seuran lehti*, *10*(1–2), 46–56.

Derobertis, J. 2018. "In Louisiana, Authorities Battle Domestic Violence Problem That's Worst than Most other States." *The Advocate*. December 22, 2018.

Dillon, N. 2018. "Mom Gets Life, Boyfriend gets Death Penalty in California Case of 'Animalistic' Child Abuse." *New York Daily News*. June 7, 2018.

Doris, T. 2018. "Just In: West Palm Mourners Hold Vigil for Slain Mother, 11-year-old Daughter." *The Palm Beach Post*. January 3, 2018.

Dorosh-Walther, B. 2014. *Out in the Night*. Fire This Time The Film.

Edelman, E. A. 2018. "Why We Forget the Pulse Nightclub Murders: Bodies That (Never) Matter and a Call for Coalitional Models of Queer and Trans Social Justice." *GLQ: A Journal of Lesbian and Gay Studies*, *24*(1), 31–35.

Emery, S. 2016. "Anaheim Man Sentenced to Prison for Transgender Woman's Murder." *The Orange County Register*. June 25, 2016.

Esquenazi, D. 2016. *Southwest of Salem: The Story of the San Antonio Four*. Esquenazi, LLC.

Fakunle, D. O., Smiley, C. J., & Gomez, M. B. 2017. "The Black President and the Black Body: The Intersection of Race, Class, Gender, and Violence in America." In *How the Obama Presidency Changed the Political Landscape*, p. 265. California: Praeger.

Farrow, Kenyon. 2016. "Silence, Omissions, and the Black Male Gay Body: HIV and the Unaccounted for Black Lives." In *2017 National Conference of Black Political Scientists (NCOBPS) Annual Meeting.* 2016.

Federal Bureau of Investigation Defining a Hate Crime. Retrieved October 2019 from https://www.fbi.gov/investigate/civil-rights/hate-crimes

Film Threat. 2013. "Bring Your Own Doc-Episode 110: "Valentine Road," HBO Documentary with Director Marta Cunningham." October 31, 2013.

Fitzgerald, K. J. 2017. "Understanding Racialized Homophobic and Transphobic Violence." In *Violence Against Black Bodies*, pp. 53–70. New York: Routledge.

Flores, A. 2014. "Transgender Woman's Mother, 'Other Family' Mourn her Death." *The Los Angeles Times.* June 24, 2014.

Fogg-Davis, H. G. (2006). "Theorizing Black Lesbians within Black Feminism: A Critique of Same-Race Street Harassment." *Politics and Gender*, 2(1), 57–76.

Follins, L., & Lassiter, J. (2016). *Black LGBT Health in the United States: The Intersection of Race, Gender, and Sexual orientation.* Maryland: Lexington Books.

Forbes, David Bruce 2003. "Mickey Mouse as Icon: Taking Popular Culture Seriously." *Word and World 23*(3), 242–252.

Franklin, K. 2002. "Good Intentions: The Enforcement of Hate Crime Penalty-Enhancement Statutes." *American Behavioral Scientist*, 46(1), 154–172.

Gares, J. 2016. *Free CeCe!* Jac Gares Media, Inc.

Gavrielides, T. 2012. "Contextualizing Restorative Justice for Hate Crime." *Journal of Interpersonal Violence*, 27(18), 3624–3643.

Gerber, M. 2018. "'Nothing Short of Evil:' Judge Sentences Mother to Life in Prison and her Boyfriend to Death in Gabriel Fernandez Murder Case." *Los Angeles Times.* June 7, 2018.

Gilliam, J. 2004. "Toward Providing a Welcoming Home for all: Enacting a New Approach to Address the Longstanding Problems Lesbian, Gay, Bisexual, and Transgender Youth Face in the Foster Care System." (Social Justice in the 21st Century). *Loyola of Los Angeles Law Review*, 37(4), 1037.

Green A., & Wong. A. 2015. "LGBT Students and Campus Sexual Assault." *The Atlantic.* September 22, 2015.

Greey, Ali. 2018. "Queer Inclusion Precludes (Black) Queer Disruption: Media Analysis of the Black Lives Matter Toronto Sit-in During Toronto Pride 2016." *Leisure Studies,* 37(6), 662–676.

Hauser, C. 2016. "Gay Man in Georgia Describes Attack with Scalding Water." *The New York Times.* March 18.

Herszenhorn. D. 2000. "Signs in Grisly Killing Point to Bias and Stepfather Who Killed Himself." *New York Times.* March 24, 2000.

Holland, A. 2006. *A Girl Like Me: The Gwen Araujo Story.* Lifetime.

Houston, W. 2018. *Toxic Silence: Race, Black Gender Identity, and Addressing the Violence against Black Transgender Women in Houston.* New York: Peter Lang, Inc.

Hutchinson, S. 2011. *Moral Combat: Black Atheists, Gender Politics, and the Values Wars.* Infidel Books.

Isoke, Zenzele. 2013. *Urban Black Women and the Politics of Resistance*. New York: Springer.

Jacobs, Michelle S. 2017. "The Violent State: Black Women's Invisible Struggle Against Police Violence." *The William and Mary Journal of Women and the Law, 24*, 39.

Jones, Robert P., Cox, Daniel, & Lienesch, Rachel. 2017. "Who sees Discrimination? Attitudes on Sexual Orientation, Gender Identity, Race, and Immigration Status: Findings from PRRI's American Values Atlas." *PRRI, June*.

Kahan, D. M. 2005. "What's Really Wrong with Shaming Sanctions." *The Texas Law Review, 84*, 2075.

Karlin, R. 2015. Schenectady, "Troy Leads States in Minority Youth Poverty." *Times Union*. March 20, 2015.

Kidd, J., & Witten, T. m. 2008. "Transgender and Transsexual Identities: The Next Strange Fruit—Hate Crimes, Violence and Genocide Against the Global Trans-Communities." *Journal of Hate Studies, 6*, 31.

King, M.L.,1968. *The Trumpet of Conscience*. New York: Harper.

Kleinknecht, William. 2005. "Man Admits to Reduced Charge in Death of Lesbian Teen," *The Star-Ledger*. March 4, 2005.

Knappenberger, Brian. 2020. *"The Trails of Gabriel Fernandez."* Luminant Media, Common Sense Media.

Kohn, S. 2001. "Greasing the Wheel: How the Criminal Justice System Hurts Gay, Lesbian, Bisexual and Transgendered People and Why Hate Crime Laws Won't Save Them." *NYU Review of Law & Social Change, 27*, 257.

Lacy, K. 2015. Race, Privilege and the Growing Class Divide. *Ethnic and Racial Studies, 38*(8), 1246–1249.

Lamont Hill, M. 2012. "Why Aren't We Fighting for CeCe McDonald?" *Ebony.com*. June 11, 2012.

Lawrence, F.M. 1999. *Punishing Hate*, Cambridge, MA: Harvard University Press.

Levin, B. 2002. "From Slavery to Hate Crime Laws: The Emergence of Race and Status-Based Protection in American Criminal Law." *Journal of Social Issues, 58*(2), 227–245.

Levy, Brian L., & Levy, Denise L. 2017. "When Love Meets Hate: The Relationship between State Policies on Gay and Lesbian Rights and Hate Crime Incidence." *Social science research, 61*, 142–159

Lewis, M. W., & Ericksen, K. S. 2016. "Improving the Climate for LGBTQ Students at an Historically Black University." *Journal of LGBT youth, 13*(3), 249–269.

Loffreda, B. 2001. *Losing Matt Shepard: Life and Politics in the Aftermath of Anti-Gay Murder*. New York: Columbia University Press.

Lohr, D. 2018. "Within 1 Week, 4 Black Lesbians were Murdered." *Queer Voices: Huffpost*. January 11, 2018.

Martos, Alexander J., Wilson, Patrick A., Gordon, Allegra R., Lightfoot, Marguerita, & Meyer, Ilan H. 2018. "Like Finding a Unicorn: Healthcare Preferences among Lesbian, Gay, and Bisexual People in the United States." *Social Science and Medicine, 208*, 126–133.

Massey, D. 2003. "Gay Pride Flag Is Raised in Newark." *Star-Ledger*. June 11, 2003.

McCann, E., & Sharek, D. 2016. "Mental Health Needs of People who Identify as Transgender: A review of the Literature." *Archives of Psychiatric Nursing, 30*(2), 280–285.

Meyer, D. 2008. "Interpreting and Experiencing Anti-Queer Violence: Race, Class, and Gender Differences among LGBT Hate Crime Victims." *Race, Gender and Class, 15*(3–4), 262–282.

Meyer, D., 2015. *Violence Against Queer People: Race, Class, Gender, and the Persistence of Anti-LGBT Discrimination.* New Jersey: Rutgers University Press.

Mogul, J. L., Ritchie, A. J., & Whitlock, K. 2011. *Queer (In) Justice: The Criminalization of LGBT People in the United States* (Vol. 5). Massachusetts: Beacon Press.

Moore, Marlon Rachquel. 2014. *In the Life and in the Spirit: Homoerotic Spirituality in African American Literature.* New York: SUNY Press.

Nadal, K. L. 2019. "Measuring LGBTQ Microaggressions: The Sexual Orientation Microaggressions Scale (SOMS) and the Gender Identity Microaggressions Scale (GIMS)." *Journal of homosexuality, 66*(10), 1404–1414.

Nadasen, P. 2004. *Welfare Warriors: The Welfare Rights Movement in the United States.* New York: Routledge.

National Gay and Lesbian Task Force. 2013. *Nondiscrimination Laws Map.* Washington, DC: National LGBTQ Task Force.

Obasogie, O. K., & Newman, Z. 2016. "Black Lives Matter and Respectability Politics in Local News Accounts of Officer-Involved Civilian Deaths: An Early Empirical Assessment." *The Wisconsin Law Review*, (3), 541– 571.

Ogles, J. 2017. "The Story Behind Pulse's Unclaimed Victim." *The Advocate.* June 8, 2017.

Parsley, J. 2019. "Two Pulse Survivors Organize March for Ex-Gays in Orlando." *South Florida News.* August, 2019.

Pascoe, C. J. 2011. *Dude, You're a Fag: Masculinity and Sexuality in High School.* California: University of California Press.

Paul, Pringle, & Saillant, Catherine. 2008. "A Deadly Clash of Emotions." 2008. *The Los Angeles Times.* March 2008.

Payne, A. A., & Welch, K. 2013. "The Impact of Schools and Education on Antisocial Behavior over the Life Course." In *Handbook of Life-Course Criminology*, pp. 93–109. New York: Springer.

Perez, N., & Torres, L. 2011. *"Latina Portrait: Latina Queer in Chicago." Beck Research Initiative for Women, Gender, and Community.* Illinois: DePaul University.

Perkiss, D. A. 2012. "A New Strategy for Neutralizing the Gay Panic Defense at Trial: Lessons from the Lawrence King Case." *The UCLA Law Review, 60*, 778.

Perry, B. 2001. *In the Name of Hate: Accounting for Hate Crime.* New York: Routledge.

Phillips, D. 2017. "Torture and killing of transgender woman stun Brazil." *The New York Times.* March 8, 2017.

Poteat, T., & Follins, L. 2016. "Narratives of Health among Black Trans Men: An Exploratory Intersectional Analysis." In *Black LGBT Health in the United States:*

The Intersection of Race, Gender, and Sexual Orientation. Maryland: Lexington Books.

Potok, M. 2000. "The Year in Hate." In *Phi Kappa Phi Forum* (Vol. 80, No. 2, p. 32). National Forum: Phi Kappa Phi Journal. April.

Prevost, M. 2010. *"Trained in the ways of men [Documentary]." United States: Reel Freedom Films.*

Puar, J. K. 2018. *Terrorist Assemblages: Homonationalism in Queer Times.* Durham: Duke University Press.

Queally, James, & Winton, Richard. 2019. "Democratic Donor Ed Buck Paid at Least 10 Men to Use Drugs for His Own Pleasure, Prosecutors Say." *Los Angeles Times.* September 19, 2019.

Quinn, K., Dickson-Gomez, J., & Young, S. 2016. "The Influence of Pastors' Ideologies of Homosexuality on HIV Prevention in the Black Church." *Journal of Religion and Health, 55*(5), 1700–1716.

Rabinowitz, P. 2015. "Street/Crime: From Rodney King's Beating to Michael Brown's Shooting." *Cultural Critique, 90*(1), 143–147.

Rachquel M. M. 2015. *In the Life and in the Spirit: Homoerotic Spirituality in African American Literature.* New York: SUNY Press.

Ramirez, J. L., Gonzalez, K. A., & Galupo, M. P. 2018. "Invisible During my own Crisis: Responses of LGBT People of Color to the Orlando Shooting." *Journal of Homosexuality, 65*(5), 579–599.

Reisner, Sari L., White Hughto, Jaclyn M., Gamarel, Kristi E., Keuroghlian, Alex S., Mizock, Lauren, & Pachankis, John E. 2016. "Discriminatory experiences associated with posttraumatic stress disorder symptoms among transgender adults." *Journal of Counseling Psychology, 63*(5), 509.

Ritchie, A. 2025. #SAYHERNAME: RACIAL PROFILING AND POLICE VIOLENCE AGAINST BLACK WOMEN. NYU School of Law.

Ross, C. J. 2015. "Bitch, Go Directly to Jail: Student Speech and Entry into the School-to-Prison Pipeline." *Temple Law Review, 88,* 717.

Rushin, S., & Edwards, G. S. 2018. The Effect of President Trump's Election on Hate Crimes. *Available at SSRN 3102652.*

Salamon, Gayle. 2018. *Life and Death of Latisha King: A Critical Phenomenology of Transphobia.* New York University Press.

Scheper-Hughes, N. 1992. *Death Without Weeping: The Violence of Everyday Life in Brazil.* University of California Press.

Sharlach, L. 1999. "Gender and Genocide in Rwanda: Women as Agents and Objects of Genocide." *Journal of Genocide Research, 1*(3), 387–399.

Snapp, Shannon D., Hoenig, Jennifer M., Fields, Amanda, & Russell, Stephen T. 2015. "Messy, Butch, and Queer: LGBTQ Youth and the School-to-Prison Pipeline." *Journal of Adolescent Research, 30*(1), 57–82.

Spade, D. 2013. "Intersectional Resistance and Law Reform." *Signs: Journal of Women in Culture and Society, 38*(4), 1031–1055.

Spade, J., & Willse, C. 2000. "Confronting the Limits of Gay Hate Crimes Activism: A Radical Critique." *Chicano-Latino Law Review, 21,* 38.

Stewart, C. 2018. *Lesbian, Gay, Bisexual, and Transgender Americans at Risk: Problems and Solutions*. California: Praeger.

Symon, E. 2020. "Mandatory Ethnic Studies Course for CSU Graduation Bill Passed by Senate." *California Globe*. June 19, 2020.

Tate, A. 2016. "Campus Pride: How Colleges Are Welcoming LGBT Students." *NBC News,* April 23, 2016.

Taylor, R. J., Chatters, L. M., & Brown, R. K. 2014. African American Religious Participation. *The Review of Religious Research*, *56*(4), 513–538.

Therolf, G. 2018. "Before his Death, 10-year-old Anthony Avalos Came Out as Gay." *Los Angeles Times.* June 26, 2018.

Thompson, S. E. 1994. *Hate groups.* New York: Lucent Books, pp. 67–79.

Vidal-Ortiz, S. 2016. "Queer-Orlando-América." *The Society Pages*. June 17, 2016.

Waldman, A. E. 2012. "All Those Like You: Identity Aggression and Student Speech." *Missouri Law Review*, *77*, 653.

Walters, M. A., Paterson, J., Brown, R., & McDonnell, L. 2017. "Hate Crimes against Trans People: Assessing Emotions, Behaviors, and Attitudes toward Criminal Justice Agencies." *Journal of Interpersonal Violence.*

West, C. 2014. "Battered, Black, and Blue: An Overview of Violence in the Lives of Black Women." In *Violence in the Lives of Black Women*, pp. 13–52. New York: Routledge.

Wilkerson I. 2014. "Mike Brown's Shooting and Jim Crow Lynchings Have Too much in Common. It's Time for America to Own Up." *The Guardian*. August 25, 2014.

Winder, T. J. 2015. "Shouting it Out:" Religion and the Development of Black Gay Identities." *Qualitative Sociology*, *38*(4), 375–394.

Young, H. 2005. "The Black Body as Souvenir in American Lynching." *Theatre Journal*, *57*(4), 639–657.

Index

About the Author

Siobhan Brooks is associate professor of African American Studies at California State University at Fullerton. Her research focuses on race, gender, identity, and sexuality. Brooks' work has been published in *The Black Scholar*, *Signs: Journal in Women and Culture and Society*, and the *Journal of Homosexuality*. She is the author of *Unequal Desires: Race and Erotic Capital in the Stripping Industry* (2010).

www.ingramcontent.com/pod-product-compliance
Lightning Source LLC
Chambersburg PA
CBHW022328280326
41932CB00010B/1262